GEORGE BUSH'S
FOREIGN AID

GEORGE BUSH'S FOREIGN AID

TRANSFORMATION *or* CHAOS?

CAROL LANCASTER

CENTER FOR GLOBAL DEVELOPMENT
Washington, D.C.

Copyright © 2008
CENTER FOR GLOBAL DEVELOPMENT
1776 Massachusetts Avenue, N.W.
Washington, D.C. 20036
www.cgdev.org

George Bush's Foreign Aid: Transformation or Chaos?
may be ordered from:
BROOKINGS INSTITUTION PRESS
c/o HFS, P.O. Box 50370, Baltimore, MD 21211-4370
Tel.: 800/537-5487; 410/516-6956; Fax: 410/516-6998; Internet: www.brookings.edu

Library of Congress Cataloging-in-Publication data

Lancaster, Carol.
   George Bush's foreign aid : transformation or chaos? / Carol Lancaster.
      p.   cm.
   Includes bibliographical references and index.
   ISBN 978-1-933286-27-3 (pbk. : alk. paper)
   1. Economic assistance, American. 2. Economic assistance, American—
Developing countries. 3. United States—Economic policy—2001– 4. United
States—Foreign economic relations—21st century. 5. Bush, George W. (George
Walker), 1946– I. Title.

   HC60.L295 2008
   338.91'7301724—dc22   2008008308

9 8 7 6 5 4 3 2 1

The paper used in this publication meets minimum requirements of the
American National Standard for Information Sciences—Permanence of Paper for
Printed Library Materials: ANSI Z39.48-1992.

Typeset in Sabon and Ocean

Composition by Cynthia Stock
Silver Spring, Maryland

Printed by Kirby Lithographic
Arlington, Virginia

Contents

Center
for Global
Development

The Center for Global Development is an independent, nonprofit policy research organization dedicated to reducing global poverty and inequality and to making globalization work for the poor. Through a combination of research and strategic outreach, the Center actively engages policymakers and the public to influence the policies of the United States, other rich countries, and such institutions as the World Bank, the IMF, and the World Trade Organization to improve the economic and social development prospects in poor countries. The Center's Board of Directors bears overall responsibility for the Center and includes distinguished leaders of nongovernmental organizations, former officials, business executives, and some of the world's leading scholars of development. The Center receives advice on its research and policy programs from the Board and from an Advisory Committee that comprises respected development specialists and advocates.

The Center's president works with the Board, the Advisory Committee, and the Center's senior staff in setting the research and program priorities and approves all formal publications. The Center is supported by an initial significant financial contribution from Edward W. Scott Jr. and by funding from philanthropic foundations and other organizations.

Preface

Since our beginnings in late 2001, my colleagues and I at the Center for Global Development have been concerned with not just more aid, but with better aid, or what has come to be called by aid insiders, "aid effectiveness." As it turns out, we have had much to consider right here in Washington. After a long period of relative dormancy in the post–cold war 1990s, aid and aid effectiveness have risen to new prominence following the 9/11 attacks and took firm hold with President Bush's announcement in March 2002 of a new approach to aid and the creation of a new implementing agency to manage it, the Millennium Challenge Corporation, and his subsequent commitment to more aid as well at a United Nations international conference later 2002 on financing development.

Starting from that moment, the Bush administration has brought, depending on your point of view and your expectations, some combination of transformation and chaos to the U.S. foreign aid system—to use the words in the title of this fine new book by one of the Center's board members and a visiting fellow, Carol Lancaster. The total volume of U.S. aid has increased in real terms, even without counting the monies that have gone to Iraq and Afghanistan. The Millennium Challenge Corporation focuses on financing programs in a highly select number of poor countries (just fifteen countries are currently eligible or close to eligible) that meet minimum standards of honest and competent government, are friendly to the business sector, and are making serious efforts to address the health, education, and other basic needs of their people. A second entirely new program, PEPFAR (the President's Emergency Program for

AIDS Relief), has put more than 1 million AIDS victims on life-sustaining medicines, again in a limited number of carefully selected poor countries. At the bureaucratic level, the U.S. Agency for International Development, the longstanding and single major U.S. aid agency (since 1961) has been increasingly integrated into the State Department, with the objective of better incorporating development into Secretary of State Condoleezza Rice's approach of "transformational diplomacy" in the world's weak and fragile states. And then there is the Pentagon, which has entered the aid business too and now finances 20 percent of all U.S. foreign aid—in this case including development programs in Iraq and Afghanistan.

Carol tells this tale, bringing to readers the politics, the bureaucracies, the people, the relations between the administration and Congress—and what has worked and what has not in the Bush administration's ambitious foreign aid effort. She also brings insight about why the changes have been transformative but chaotic—and wisdom about the lessons for shaping a better approach in the next administration.

Carol's book follows in a series of books and other contributions of CGD staff in the last six years on aid, aid effectiveness, and in particular on U.S. programs. These include Steven Radelet on the Millennium Challenge Account (*Challenging Foreign Aid: A Policymaker's Guide to the Millennium Challenge Account,* 2003), Ruth Levine on major aid-financed public health programs of proven effectiveness (*Millions Saved: Proven Successes in Global Health,* 2004), a CGD commission report on the shortcomings of the U.S. approach to weak and fragile states (*On the Brink, Weak States and US National Security,* 2004), and ongoing analyses of MCC and PEPFAR implementation by our staff in MCA and HIV/AIDS Monitor programs, and dozens of papers available at (www.cgdev.org/content/publications/).

This book is an easy, even exciting, read. I am confident it will find a broad and influential readership among scholars, advocates, practitioners, and policymakers—and not only in the United States, but in old and new donor countries, including Europe, Australia and Canada, China, and the Middle East.

NANCY BIRDSALL
President
Center for Global Development
Washington, D.C.

Acknowledgments

I wish to thank the Center for Global Development for supporting the research, writing, and publication of this book. In particular, thanks go to Nancy Birdsall, president of the Center, for her support and encouragement. In my experience, books almost never come out the way they are planned. That was the case with this book as well. I began the research with a number of ideas about the subject matter, but in the process of interviewing, I revised substantially my perception of the purposes and trajectories of the many changes in U.S. aid during the Bush administration. I wish to thank the many individuals in government whom I have been able to interview for this book. Their insights were, as one would expect, not always consistent with one another. But all have been extremely valuable and have, without doubt, improved the quality of this book. Since many of them asked that their names not be included in the acknowledgments, I will respect their wishes and not mention anyone in a public position at the time of this writing. Thanks to David Gartner and Bob Lester for their insights as well.

Thanks also to those who read the manuscript and made very useful comments: Gerry Hyman, Barbara Turner, George Ingram, Steve Radelet, Sheila Herrling, Ruth Levine, Jennifer Windsor, Andrew Natsios, Dennis Detray, Stewart Patrick, Ed Scott, Princeton Lyman, and Laura Wilson. Special thanks to Laura for writing a box in the book on the rationale for improved data collection in the F process reforms.

This book owes much to those who shared their knowledge, experience and insights with me. Any shortcomings belong to me.

ONE

Introduction

O ver the past seven years, the Bush administration has launched a transformation of U.S. foreign aid. No time since the administration of President John F. Kennedy has seen more changes in the volume of aid, in aid's purposes and policies, in its organization, and in its overall status in U.S. foreign policy. If "transformation" in politics is taken to mean fundamentally changing existing systems, President Bush has initiated one.

But the notion of "transformation" also implies radical change in pursuit of a broad new vision. Such a vision has been absent from the numerous changes in aid implemented by the Bush administration, leaving an aid system—already in considerable disarray—in chaos. However, the policy and organizational chaos characterizing U.S. aid offers the next administration an important and compelling opportunity to reshape U.S. economic assistance while engaging the emerging world of the twenty-first century.[1]

The view that U.S. aid in 2008 is badly in need of policy and organizational reform is reflected in the veritable blizzard of books, study commission statements, and congressional reports on aid published in recent years, especially in 2007 (see box 1-1). These efforts share a number of common concerns though the specifics of their policy recommendations are quite different.

These reports and studies reflect the extraordinary interest combined with considerable disquiet about foreign aid in the foreign policy and

1

BOX 1-1. Books and Reports on Foreign Aid, Development, and Foreign Policy

Beyond Assistance, HELP Commission Report on Foreign Assistance Reform (2007)

Commission on Smart Power (Center for Strategic and International Studies, 2007)

Embassies Grapple to Guide Foreign Aid, A Report to Members of the Committee on Foreign Relations, United States Senate, November 16, 2007, 110 Cong. 1st sess.

Integrating 21st Century Development and Security Assistance, Final Report of the Task Force on Nontraditional Security Assistance (Center for Strategic and International Studies, 2008)

On the Brink: Commission on Weak States and US National Security (Center for Global Development, 2004)

Security by Other Means, Lael Brainard, ed. (Brookings, 2006)

Major Concerns and Recommendations

◆ Need to elevate development as key element in U.S. foreign policy to support U.S. interests, values, and leadership in the world
◆ Need for overall vision of the role of foreign aid
◆ Need for greater focus on a limited number of goals for the use of aid
◆ Concern about the impact of the Department of Defense in the aid and development business
◆ Need for reform to overcome problems of organizational fragmentation and disarray in aid system
◆ Need to better explain to the American people the objectives and importance of foreign aid/development

---

development communities. They mostly examine foreign aid from a particular policy perspective—for example, its relation to security or broader foreign policy issues or fragile states. This study adds to the aid discussion by examining U.S. economic assistance as a whole, analyzing in detail the array of recent reforms and the difficult issues they raise, and placing these changes and the manner of their implementation in a historical and political context. It agrees with many of the reports and commissions that a major reform in U.S. foreign aid is urgently required, including elevating "development" in U.S. foreign policy in reality as well as in rhetoric. It considers the creation of a Department for Development has much to recommend it. But it also recognizes that a Department for Development is controversial, especially in the foreign policy community, and could be politically costly and time consuming to plan and implement for a new administration. It thus offers a "Plan B" that would improve the existing system but imply fewer political costs for a new administration, which will inherit a large number of urgent and difficult problems, domestic and foreign, that it will have to confront once in office.

Elements of a Transformation: Changes in U.S. Foreign Aid

Foreign aid is an instrument of U.S. foreign policy and sometimes of U.S. domestic policy. It is used to pursue a variety of national purposes, including providing humanitarian relief, furthering diplomatic goals, promoting development and democracy abroad, addressing global issues, supporting economic and political transitions, expanding export markets, preventing and mitigating conflict, and strengthening weak states. Of all of these, promoting diplomacy and development have long been the most prominent purposes of U.S. aid, reflecting U.S. interests and values abroad and sustaining an often uneasy coalition of domestic support for aid-giving from the political right and left within the United States.

It is worth considering what I mean here by "diplomacy" and "development" as purposes of U.S. economic assistance. Strictly speaking, *diplomacy* includes the tools and tactics used to shape relations between countries. In this study, I shall take the liberty of using the term somewhat differently—to refer to the issues in U.S. relations with other countries that relate to U.S. national interests (primarily security and political interests) and U.S. leadership abroad. The specific diplomatic goals for which U.S. economic assistance has been used include containing the spread of communism, promoting peace (for example, in the Middle East and the Balkans) and fighting the global war on terror. In addressing these issues, U.S. aid has been used to strengthen friendly governments and their economies, to reward desirable behavior (for example, the provision of base rights, votes in the United Nations, support of U.S. policies generally) and to secure the U.S. presence, access, and influence worldwide. I shall use *development* to refer to rising levels of per capita income and reductions in poverty with all the complex changes, including improved health and education, robust political institutions, high levels of savings, investment and trade, and other social, political, and economic changes that are both causes and consequences of development.[2]

Aid for development has been used to expand the capacity of developing country governments to manage their economies (for example, through technical assistance and training), to increase assets supportive of development (for example, through funding increased infrastructure, health, education, credit, agricultural support), and to act as an incentive for governments to adopt economic and political reforms regarded as essential to foster investment, growth, and poverty reduction.

In the 1990s, with the end of the cold war, the value of aid as an instrument of diplomacy diminished, and with growing doubts about its effectiveness in furthering development (especially in Africa), the importance of aid and of promoting development abroad declined, along with the volume of that aid.

President Bush dramatically reversed both of these trends. In his two major statements on the national security strategy of the United States, he dedicated one or more sections to development, signaling that it is in the first tier of U.S. foreign policy priorities, along with defense and diplomacy.[3] This is the first time for many decades that a U.S. president has declared that promoting development abroad is a key priority in U.S. foreign policy. And the major instrument of that policy was inevitably foreign aid.[4]

Following these statements, the *volume* of U.S. aid has grown dramatically during the Bush administration—faster than at any time since the Marshall Plan. In current dollars, U.S. aid was higher in 2005 (and slightly down in 2006, the last year for which data are available, see figures 1-1, 1-2) than at any time in U.S. history, even deducting the monies for reconstruction in Iraq and Afghanistan and aid to Pakistan (figure 1-3).[5] (The light bars—series 2 in figure 1-3—represent aid to Pakistan, Iraq and Afghanistan.)

This increase has lifted the United States out of bottom place on the list of governments providing aid as a percentage of Gross National Income (GNI)—a position it occupied for many years. (However, it is still only one rung from the bottom.)[6]

The purposes governing U.S. aid also changed during the Bush administration. Aid for diplomatic purposes now includes fighting the global

F I G U R E   1 - 1.   U.S. Foreign Aid, 1946–2006[a]

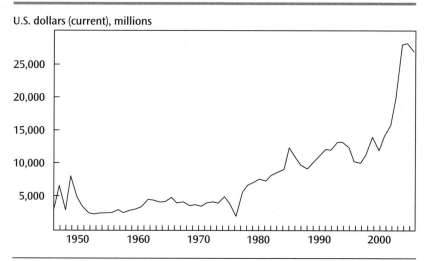

U.S. dollars (current), millions

Source: U.S. Agency for International Development (USAID), *U.S. Overseas Loans and Grants* (Greenbook) (http://qesdb.usaid.gov/gbk/index.html).

a. If one deducts funds spent on Iraq reconstruction during 2004–05 (amounting to $6 billion in 2004 and $10 billion in 2005), these increases in U.S. aid are still significant.

F I G U R E   1 - 2.   U.S. Aid in Constant Dollars, 1946–2006[a]

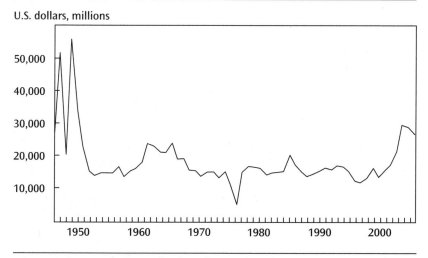

U.S. dollars, millions

Source: U.S. Agency for International Development (USAID), *U.S. Overseas Loans and Grants* (Greenbook) (http://qesdb.usaid.gov/gbk/index.html).

a. In constant dollars, U.S. aid between 2004 and 2006 was larger than at any time since the Marshall Plan.

F I G U R E 1 - 3. U.S. Aid for Afghanistan, Iraq, Pakistan, and Others, 1997–2006

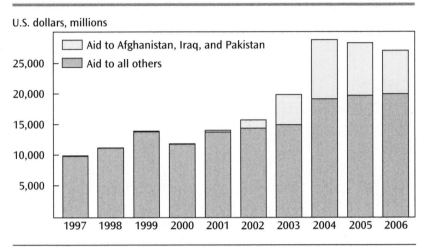

U.S. dollars, millions

Source: U.S. Agency for International Development (USAID), *U.S. Overseas Loans and Grants* (Greenbook) (http://qesdb.usaid.gov/gbk/index.html).

F I G U R E 1 - 4. Net ODA as a Percentage of GNI, 2006

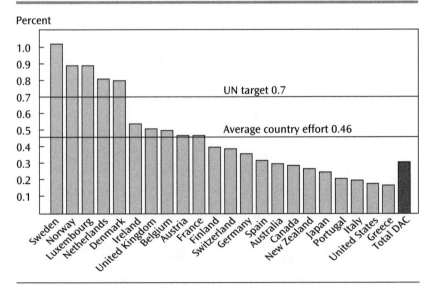

Percent

Source: Development Assistance Committee (DAC), Organization for Economic Cooperation and Development (www.oecd.org/dataoecd/23/14/37955301.pdf).
GNI: gross national income.
ODA: official development aid.

war on terror.[7] And there has been a dramatic increase in aid for global health, especially fighting HIV/AIDS—a use of aid that is aimed at addressing a global issue but has great relevance for development in poor countries as well.

Changes in aid in the Bush administration have involved the way the U.S. government organizes itself to manage its aid. An entirely new aid agency has been established—the Millennium Challenge Corporation (MCC). There has been an integration of planning and budgeting by the U.S. Agency for International Development (USAID) and the Department of State. The President's Emergency Program for AIDS Relief (PEPFAR)— a new aid program to fight HIV/AIDS—is up and running. And the Department of Defense (DoD) has become increasingly prominent in providing economic assistance, with every sign that that prominence will continue to grow.

Two new approaches to delivering aid have been implemented. One, led by the MCC, involves performance-based aid—providing relatively large amounts of aid to countries that are deemed "good performers" to spur their economic growth. And to ensure ownership of aid-funded activities, the recipients must take an active role in deciding how the aid is to be spent. A second approach, led by PEPFAR, involves applying very large amounts of aid ($30 billion for the coming five years) to tackle a single major problem: the scourge of HIV/AIDS. Aid monies have been used to address a variety of functional or global problems in the past, but never has the amount of aid allocated to PEPFAR been used against a single world problem in the space of a relatively short period of time.

Each of these changes in U.S. aid giving has much to recommend it. Elevating the promotion of development abroad as a priority in U.S. foreign policy reflects the realities of the twenty-first century in which massive disparities in wealth and opportunity in a rapidly integrating world can generate serious threats to U.S. interests abroad and the well-being of Americans at home. Addressing the problems of poverty abroad as a priority of U.S. foreign policy also reflects the values and views of many Americans that they, being among the most blessed and wealthy of peoples in human history, should act to help bring those blessings to the 2 billion of the world's population living in severe deprivation. Further, giving development a central place in foreign policy strengthens U.S. leadership in the world by combining "soft power"—the ability to attract and persuade others to do what you want (often through demonstrating that you have their interests at heart as well as yours)—with "hard power"—threats, sometimes involving the use of force, to compel compliance from others. And expanding the volume of U.S. aid dramatically brings it to a level more consistent with international needs, with the U.S. role as the world's sole superpower, and with the ability of the United States to provide international economic assistance.[8]

With regard to the aid policy and programmatic initiatives of the Bush administration, the approach of the MCC to aid giving—preferring those countries whose governments performed well in promoting democracy and development—has been welcomed with its promise of more effective aid in support of more rapid development. The large increase in U.S. aid to fight HIV/AIDS—one of the worst plagues to afflict humanity for many centuries—has been very well received by groups and individuals from all points on the political spectrum. The State Department–USAID integration of aid budget and policy planning was seen by many as a useful reform that would enhance the coherence of U.S. aid giving and align it more closely with U.S. foreign policy. The rise of the DoD as an aid-giving agency and, in particular, the creation of AFRICOM (a new military command for Africa) have been regarded as innovations justified by the problems of fighting terrorism generally as well as the difficulties of managing community relations during U.S. military occupations.

At the same time, a number of theses changes have raised serious concerns. The MCC has been extraordinarily slow in disbursing the sizeable amount of funding appropriated to it, raising questions about the efficacy of this new model of performance and ownership-based aid giving. There is some evidence that large amounts of funding for HIV/AIDS have begun to have negative effects on other efforts to address health conditions abroad and may simply be too large for recipients to absorb quickly and effectively. More basically, the massive increase in aid for HIV/AIDS skews overall U.S. bilateral aid away from development, which requires addressing many obstacles impeding economic progress in poor countries, including limited health care. The integration of USAID and Department of State planning and budgeting has sowed confusion and discontent in both agencies and raises fear in the development community that aid programs will eventually focus more on short-term diplomatic goals, and not the longer-term development mission of USAID. The increasing engagement of the DoD in aid giving adds yet another big player to a cluttered landscape of aid organizations in the U.S. government, a player with, as yet, no professional capacity to manage aid for stabilization and development and that can give the impression of a militarization of U.S. foreign aid.

Finally, in addition to the substance of the changes, there has been considerable controversy about the ideas behind some of them (such as the "failing states" paradigm), their organizational implications, and the manner in which some of them have been implemented.

This book offers a stocktaking and analysis of U.S. foreign aid as it has changed since 2000 and offers recommendations for its future. It examines the principal changes in four chapters: first, it describes the individual changes themselves, including their origins, their promise, and their potential problems; second, it analyzes several major policy issues raised by the changes; third, it examines the organizational issues raised by the reforms and the problems in their implementation, including change management in the public sector; fourth, the book concludes with a look at the evolving context of aid giving in the twenty-first century and recommends a set of changes in U.S. aid to meet the opportunities and challenges of the new world of aid giving.

The message of this study is simple: first, foreign aid is an essential instrument of U.S. foreign policy, broadly defined, and will remain so for the foreseeable future; second, initiatives over the past seven years have produced both a transformation *and* chaos in an aid system that was already in disarray and ripe for change. The next administration must address the challenge and opportunity of keeping what is valuable in these changes, discarding what is not working, and melding these initiatives into a coherent vision of the role of foreign aid and U.S. foreign policy. In short, it has the chance to complete a transformation of U.S. aid.

TWO

The Changing Landscape of U.S. Foreign Aid

At the end of the twentieth century, U.S. foreign aid, and the U.S. Agency for International Development (USAID), looked like they might be heading toward extinction. The cold war was over. It had long been an important rationale for U.S. aid giving—one that helped sustain an uneasy right-left coalition supporting annual aid appropriations. The political right in the United States, which tended to be hostile to foreign aid, acquiesced to aid giving when it was tied to national security issues; the left was increasingly less impressed with national security rationales for aid but supported it as a means of promoting development and helping to reduce poverty abroad. For many years, this tenuous coalition was the lynchpin of U.S. foreign aid in Congress and elsewhere. Peace making in the Middle East, beginning in the mid-1970s and involving large-scale aid to Israel and Egypt, had also been a basis for broad support for foreign assistance across the political spectrum. With an agreement in the mid-1990s to gradually eliminate economic assistance to Israel and reduce assistance to Egypt by half, this domestic political basis for U.S. aid giving also threatened to erode.

During the 1990s, small wars and civil conflicts proliferated in Africa, the Balkans, and Russia's "near abroad," but few of these presented significant challenges to U.S. security.[1] They did, however, create serious humanitarian crises and development failures. Global problems such as the transmission of infectious diseases, climate change, and environmental degradation were of growing prominence but not generally seen as immediate threats to Americans' well-being and so did not constitute new, compelling security rationales for U.S. aid.[2]

With regard to the development purpose of aid, there was increasing disillusionment with the effectiveness of economic assistance in furthering growth and poverty reduction—above all in sub-Saharan Africa, where the development challenges were most difficult and the apparent impact of large amounts of aid over several decades had been disappointing.

These changes in the 1990s in the world of U.S. aid giving made it easier for the Clinton administration to cut U.S. aid programs, contained within discretionary government spending, as part of an effort to balance the federal budget.[3] However, after declining steadily from the early years of the decade, foreign aid began to rise slowly by the end of the 1990s, spurred by responses to humanitarian disasters abroad, such as Hurricane Mitch in Central America. Increases were also urged by nongovernmental organizations (NGOs) and elements of the foreign policy community at home, claiming that the United States was in danger of losing an important foreign policy tool and turning its back on the needy abroad.

During this period, the principal U.S. bilateral aid agency—USAID—looked into an uncertain future. The agency had become unpopular in Washington, though it was quite well regarded by U.S. embassy staff and aid agencies of other governments in the field.[4] Almost since its creation in 1961, it had been the target of criticisms from members of Congress and others opposed to aid giving abroad or skeptical that such aid could promote growth in poor countries. Criticizing foreign aid was also used as a means for attacking the administration when such aid supported an unpopular program abroad (for example, aid in support of the contras in Central America during the mid-1980s). Additionally, criticisms came from nongovernmental organizations working in relief and development, which found USAID difficult to deal with, and from agencies within the executive branch that complained often that USAID was slow and unresponsive.

There was some justification for these critiques, though many of the problems confronting USAID were beyond its control. The agency had myriads of complex and time-consuming regulations that it followed in planning and programming its monies. These regulations were not, however, entirely self-generated. Some came from Congress itself in the form of earmarks or directives on how USAID could or could not spend its funding. Some came from efforts on the part of the administration to ensure that funds were competed for fairly and spent cleanly (which a series of inspectors general monitored assiduously). Others reflected USAID's own efforts to avoid being publicly pilloried for making embarrassing mistakes in its expenditures abroad. USAID also used its complicated and opaque regulations to keep other executive branch agencies from raiding its budget (which they frequently tried to do), giving it the reputation of being "difficult to deal with."[5] Rightly or wrongly, these critiques contributed to the fragmentation of U.S. foreign aid; under successive administrations, authorities for new spending programs abroad for activities similar to those funded by USAID were located in other agencies. For example, coordinators for aid to Eastern Europe and the former Soviet Union were situated in the Department of State; a growing democracy funding program was located there; and small assistance programs were established in nearly all federal departments.[6] This fragmentation eventually began to raise concerns about the coherence, overlap, and duplication in U.S. aid efforts abroad.

In short, at the beginning of the administration of George W. Bush, there was a widely shared view that it was long past time for a major reform of the U.S. system of aid giving and in the organization of U.S. foreign affairs agencies generally.

Reforming U.S. Aid: Past Experience

No matter how much need there has been for reform in the system of aid giving, major changes in the volume and organization of U.S. aid have never been easy. Such changes typically involve gaining a measure of consensus within administrations for change, usually in the face of resistance from those bureaucracies whose interests may be gored. Then there is the challenge of obtaining enough support from Congress, especially where new legislation is required—not easy when members of Congress are tempted to add extraneous or unwelcome amendments to legislation involving a program as controversial as foreign aid and one that lacks a constituency coherent enough and strong enough to fend off such amendments. Finally, proposed changes must garner the support of the many outside interests associated with foreign aid programs, which typically all have connections with members of Congress and elements of the bureaucracy, and so can be ignored by an administration only at a potentially high political cost. In short, presidents and administration officials usually have to spend considerable political capital to bring about major changes in aid programs or, for that matter, in any major federal program.

The last significant organizational reform involving foreign aid took place in 1961, when the Kennedy administration combined several separate aid programs into the new USAID. These changes were the result of planning by the administration to make U.S. aid policies more coherent and the organization of aid more rational and reflective of those policies. It was decided then that U.S. bilateral aid should be semi-independent of the Department of State, intended, as it was, to serve both U.S. foreign policy and development interests abroad. Kennedy got his legislation through Congress but did not get all he wanted. For example, his proposal to locate the Peace Corps within USAID was turned down, and it remains independent today.

Major efforts to reform U.S. aid have since occurred more or less every decade. In the early 1970s, President Nixon decided to divide USAID into three separate agencies according to their function, with one to specialize in managing research and technical assistance, one to manage aid loans, and the third to coordinate aid, trade, and investment in developing countries. This complicated proposal for reform never got anywhere in Congress, and the president did not put much effort into pushing it.

In 1973 Congress passed legislation bringing about a major reform of U.S. aid that involved policy rather than organizational change: aid was reoriented toward providing for the basic human needs of those in poor countries—primary health care, basic education, shelter, agricultural assistance for small farmers. This reform was led by powerful and committed members of Congress, who were able to drive their authorizing legislation intact through the House International Affairs and the Senate Foreign Relations committees. Since 1985 the House International Affairs Committee and the Senate Foreign Relations Committee have failed to pass a single aid reauthorization bill.

In the late 1970s, Senator Hubert Humphrey introduced legislation to create an International Development Cooperation Agency (IDCA) to bring more coherence to U.S. development programs abroad, including bilateral aid, multilateral aid (the responsibility for which is lodged in the U.S. Treasury), and foreign investment promotion activities (for which the Overseas Private Investment Corporation was responsible). Senator Humphrey died before the legislation was passed, but the Carter administration took up the idea and created an IDCA considerably weaker than what the senator had envisioned—one which only had the power of coordination among these separate programs. In the end, having no control over the personnel or budgets of the agencies it was supposed to coordinate, IDCA was resisted, ignored, and eventually eliminated.[7]

Yet another effort to reform the U.S. aid system was initiated by Congress in the late 1980s. This time the reform effort concentrated on rewriting the basic legislative basis for U.S. foreign aid—the Foreign Assistance Act of 1961, amended so many times that the entire act is more than 500 pages long. This effort, led by Representatives Lee Hamilton and Benjamin Gilman, attempted to streamline processes and concentrate the focus of aid giving on a limited number of priorities. As their legislation moved through Congress, it picked up so many amendments that it became unwieldy and finally unacceptable to the administration of President George H. W. Bush. It too failed.

These four attempts to reform aid giving were aimed primarily at making aid for development more effective and addressing public and congressional criticisms of U.S. aid programs. As for the changes proposed in the Nixon and Carter administrations and the Hamilton-Gilman effort, proponents of these changes underestimated the difficulties of getting acceptable legislation on foreign aid out of Congress, and successive presidents were unwilling to spend the political capital necessary to get such legislation. The basic human needs legislation succeeded because it had support from several key members of Congress, from the administration, and from the development community, reflecting a widely shared view that it was time for a more developmental focus in U.S. aid in the wake of its use in the war in Indochina to prop up governments there. There was, in effect, what scholars like to call "an open window" for change in which a policy problem is widely recognized, a solution is available, and there are political leaders in key places willing to drive a change.[8]

An effort initiated by the Department of State in 1994 to merge USAID into the Department of State also failed. The secretary of state proposed to Vice President Gore that as part of Gore's "reinventing government" efforts, a study be undertaken of the pros and cons of such a merger, and the vice president agreed. As a defensive measure, USAID produced its own version of the merger as an option for this study that proposed that several aid programs within the Department of State—such as aid for refugees, democracy, and population—be shifted to USAID.[9]

After a campaign by USAID that involved efforts to mobilize the media, the NGOs, Congress, and other potential allies within the administration, which were few but included one powerful one—First Lady Hillary Clinton, who had become a fan of USAID's development work after visiting a number of its projects in South Asia, Africa, and Latin America—the vice president decided against a merger. Rather, USAID would "take foreign policy guidance from the Secretary of State," which it was already doing. This decision changed little in the way USAID and State related to one another in aid matters.[10] It was presented as more of a change than it actually was, partly as a way of saving face for the secretary of state who had lost the merger battle with USAID.[11]

These efforts to reorganize the U.S. system of foreign aid illustrate the dilemma of major organizational and policy reforms: fundamental reform typically provokes resistance and is almost always politically costly and time consuming as executive branch agencies, Congress, and relevant interests have to be overridden, bought off with concessions elsewhere, or brought on board and kept on board—and the bigger the reform and the more legislative changes needed, the more costly and time consuming the process. It is seldom possible to get acceptable legislation involving such changes through Congress without the active and sustained engagement of the president and other senior administration officials as well as key leaders in Congress.

U.S. Aid in the Bush Administration

In addition to the major increase in the volume of aid monies, President Bush has sought to implement the most ambitious set of changes in the organization and purposes of U.S. aid since the Kennedy administration. The first major change was the creation in 2003 of the Millennium Challenge Corporation (MCC)—an entirely new aid agency intended to provide economic assistance to governments of low-income countries who were "good performers." The second change was to establish the President's Emergency Program for AIDS Response (PEPFAR), announced in 2003. This program is managed by a coordinator with the rank of ambassador who reports to the secretary of state. The third change, announced in 2005, was the new policy of "transformational diplomacy." This included the "dual hatting" of the USAID administrator as director of U.S. foreign assistance, a new role that gave the administrator authority over not only the USAID budget, but foreign assistance budgets located in the Department of State as well. The USAID administrator/director of U.S. foreign assistance was to report to the secretary of state. Fourth, there has been the gradual expansion of economic aid programs run by the Department of Defense (representing over 20 percent of U.S. economic assistance in 2005),[12] which includes reconstruction aid for Iraq and Afghanistan but promises to go beyond these conflict-related aid programs to become a more general source of funding for stabilization and community development projects throughout the world.

The Millennium Challenge Corporation

The MCC arose out of the United Nations Conference on Financing Development held in Monterrey, Mexico, in March 2002. President Bush could not avoid attending this conference since his friend and neighbor, President Vicente Fox of Mexico, was hosting it. Having decided to attend, the president then had to have a "deliverable"—something important and attractive to announce, and the only thing that made sense was an increase in U.S. aid, the more so because European leaders were already planning on announcing significant increases in their own aid budgets. The Monterrey conference acted as a trigger for an increase in aid that, reportedly, some in the administration had already been planning.

President Bush's decision to increase U.S. aid by $5 billion per year by 2006 through a new Millennium Challenge Account (MCA) was influenced by the rock musician Bono. While he looks like a rock star—sun glasses, slightly unshaven, black t-shirts, jeans, and jacket—Bono is a most unusual one: he is passionate about development and poverty reduction, especially in Africa. And as a devout Christian, he had access to a number

President Bush speaking at the Inter-American Development Bank, March 14, 2002. Seated on stage from left to right are Bono, Cardinal McCarrick of Washington, D.C., and James Wolfensohn, president of the World Bank. Source: White House (www.whitehouse.gov/news/releases/2002/03/images/20020314-7-1.html).

of influential religious conservatives in Washington, including President George Bush, whom he is said to have lobbied effectively for a generous increase in U.S. aid. While this story has not been fully told, government officials at that time confirm that Bono's role was very influential.[13] In addition, a picture of President Bush making a preliminary announcement of the increase in U.S. aid at the Inter-American Development Bank just before the Monterrey meeting shows Bono on stage with the president, and he was one of those whom the president thanked in his remarks.

A proposed increase in foreign aid by $5 billion per year would have been risky at almost any time in the previous fifty years. Congress almost certainly would have balked, and many foreign aid critics would have joined budget hawks in attacking and defeating such a proposal. But 2002 was not just any time. It was shortly after 9/11 when the American people were painfully aware that problems and discontent in one part of the world could produce dire consequences at home. With both houses of Congress controlled by Republicans and with Democrats and the media reluctant to oppose the president in the wake of the terrorist attack and

TABLE 2-1. Millennium Challenge Corporation Indicators

Indicator	Category	Source
Civil liberties	Ruling justly	Freedom House
Political rights	Ruling justly	Freedom House
Voice and accountability	Ruling justly	World Bank Institute
Government effectiveness	Ruling justly	World Bank Institute
Rule of law	Ruling justly	World Bank Institute
Control of corruption	Ruling justly	World Bank Institute
Immunization rate	Investing in people	World Health Organization
Public expenditure on health	Investing in people	World Health Organization
Girls' primary education completion rate	Investing in people	UNESCO
Public expenditure on primary education	Investing in people	UNESCO and national sources
Cost of starting a business	Economic freedom	International Finance Corporation
Inflation rate	Economic freedom	IMF WEO
Days to start a business	Economic freedom	International Finance Corporation
Trade policy	Economic freedom	Heritage Foundation
Regulatory quality	Economic freedom	World Bank Institute
Fiscal policy	Economic freedom	National sources, cross-checked with IMF WEO
Natural resource management index	Supplemental information	CIESIN/Yale
Land rights and access index	Supplemental information	IFAD and International Finance Corporation

Source: MCC website (www.mcc.gov/selection/indicators/index.php).
CIESIN: Center for International Earth Science Information Network; IFAD: International Fund for Agricultural Development; IMF WEO: International Monetary Fund's World Economic Outlook database; UNESCO: United Nations Educational, Scientific and Cultural Organization.

the emerging global war on terror, Congress was more than willing to support the president's proposal for a substantial increase in aid.

Finally, to counter arguments that aid had been ineffective, the president tied aid to the performance of recipient governments, arguing that good policy performance would produce more effective aid. Those that "govern justly, invest in their people, and encourage economic freedom" would be eligible to receive the new aid and arguably make the most effective use of it. Decisions on eligibility would be based primarily on sixteen objective indicators of performance—since increased to eighteen—such as the control of corruption, costs of starting a business, and expenditures on public health. Table 2-1 shows the eighteen indicators, where they fit into the general criteria for MCA aid, and where the data come from in applying the indicators.

Multiyear commitments of substantial amounts of aid to low-income (and later also to middle-income) countries based on these eligibility requirements were intended to provide incentives for countries to adopt policy reforms that would establish their eligibility. Up to 10 percent of the MCA funding was also authorized for threshold countries—to help those countries close to qualifying for funding but still lacking in certain areas to implement the reforms that would make them eligible. Additionally, recipient governments would play a major role in deciding how the aid was used in their countries by preparing and submitting funding requests that reflected their priorities.

The use of objective indicators to determine eligibility for U.S. aid was intended to take the guesswork, and U.S. diplomatic and political priorities, out of aid allocation decisions. The emphasis on having the recipient government play the major role in deciding how to use the aid was intended to ensure that the aid was "owned" by that government—that is, that recipient governments had a commitment and vested interest in the aid's being effective and its outputs sustainable. Both of these approaches had been much talked about in the past and on occasion made part of individual aid-funded activities, but they were never implemented as a core element in U.S. bilateral assistance. Together, they made the MCA an innovative approach to U.S. aid giving and, it was expected, would create incentives for other governments to become good performers to qualify for MCC aid. This was what came to be called the "MCC effect." Additional innovations included the absence of congressional earmarks on MCA authorization and appropriations legislation and the ability of recipients of MCA funds to purchase goods and services from providers outside the United States. (USAID funding was estimated to be around 70 percent tied to U.S.-produced goods and services in the Clinton administration; the percentage of tied aid is no longer published.)

A decision had to be made as to where the MCA would be located bureaucratically. Would it be part of USAID, as many, including USAID administrator Andrew Natsios, expected? Would it be located in the Department of State, as was reportedly urged by Secretary of State Colin Powell? In the end, the president chose to create an entirely new aid agency, the Millennium Challenge Corporation, to manage the new monies. The reason for this decision was not made public. It could be conjectured that the MCA was not located at State because it was supposed to be a program-based agency, focused on development rather than diplomatic priorities. The State Department had limited experience running this type of program, and it was not in the development business. Locating the MCA in USAID might put at risk the innovative approach to aid giving intended for the MCA, which differed from USAID's more traditional approach of playing a major role in managing the design and implementation of aid activities itself. Putting the MCA in USAID might also tempt Congress to extend its practice of earmarking USAID's appropriations to those of the MCA. And as noted earlier, USAID did not have a strong reputation in Washington for effectiveness or responsiveness, especially among the conservatives who populated the Bush administration; thus, support for its location there may have been limited among those making or influencing the decision.

The MCC was formally established in January 2004 as an independent, subcabinet-level agency with a chief executive officer and a board of directors that included the secretaries of state and the Treasury, the USAID administrator, the special trade representative, the CEO of the MCC, and four public members appointed by the administration and approved by the Senate. The new agency got off to a rocky start. It took a considerable amount of time to staff up, even though the number of staff was quite small—100 at first but reaching 300 at the time of this writing. And though much of the staff hired in the first year came with plenty of experience in finance, banking, and law, many had limited experience in development or in operating a government spending program. The MCC specifically avoided dealing with USAID (reportedly leadership and staff were fearful of being absorbed by that agency if it collaborated too closely) and lost an opportunity to learn from USAID's extensive experience in managing assistance programs and using its in-country expertise.[14]

It took even longer for the MCC to identify eligible countries and negotiate the multiyear compacts with them that would lay out the activities to be funded with MCC aid and indicate the expected results. The compacts themselves had to be developed by the recipient government in consultation with its own civil society and private sector. And an "accountable entity" had to be set up within recipient countries (governed by a board of responsible individuals from that country) to manage the MCC funds.

By June 2005, a year and a half after it was established, the MCC had made little progress, having approved only two compacts and having disbursed almost no money. After a number of African leaders complained to President Bush that the MCC had provided them little aid thus far, Paul Applegarth, the CEO of the corporation, resigned (or was asked to leave) and a new CEO, John Danilovich, was named. By the end of 2007, activity had picked up with fifteen country compacts signed along with thirteen threshold compacts. However, disbursements still remained limited and well below projected levels, amounting to only $125 million out of $4.8 billion in commitments.[15] Just under half of the $4.8 billion was in commitments signed in 2007. But even for those MCC country programs that had been under way for several years—signed in 2006 or before—disbursements were equal to only 5 percent of a total of $2.3 billion, and almost all of those programs were well under anticipated annual spending levels. The list below shows the countries that have signed compacts with the MCC and their implementation status as of November 2007:

- ◆ Armenia: Implementing
- ◆ Benin: Implementing
- ◆ Cape Verde: Implementing
- ◆ El Salvador: Signed 2007
- ◆ Georgia: Implementing
- ◆ Ghana: Signed 2006
- ◆ Honduras: Implementing
- ◆ Lesotho: Signed 2007
- ◆ Madagascar: Implementing
- ◆ Mali: Signed 2006
- ◆ Mongolia: Signed 2007
- ◆ Morocco: Signed 2007
- ◆ Mozambique: Signed 2007
- ◆ Nicaragua: Implementing
- ◆ Vanuatu: Implementing

The slow rate was troubling to MCC leadership and members of Congress who were reluctant to appropriate the full president's budget requests for the agency until they saw more monies actually being disbursed and results assessed. The Senate Committee on Appropriations reflected these concerns in its June 2007 report on appropriations for fiscal year 2008:

> The slow rate of disbursement reflects, in part, the MCC's overly optimistic estimates of compact countries' capacity to meet compact requirements, which may result in significant unobligated but undisbursed balances when compacts expire. There are few tangible results that can be measured from any of these compacts."[16]

Under current legislation, if obligations included in the compacts are not expended by the end of the five-year compact period, these funds will be lost, leaving planned projects unfinished and creating an impression of failure at home. Despite the slowness of its beginning operations, the MCC was regarded as a potentially valuable innovation in U.S. aid giving. The MCC is due to be reauthorized in 2008 when questions about its performance and its impact will be front and center.

President's Emergency Plan for AIDS Relief (PEPFAR)

At his State of the Union speech in January 2003, President Bush made a surprise announcement—he would ask Congress for $15 billion to be spent over five years to fight HIV/AIDS worldwide. While the federal government was already funding HIV/AIDS programs abroad, the size of the president's proposed increase in funding was astonishing and well received at home and abroad. In June 2007 President Bush proposed a doubling in PEPFAR funding—to $30 billion over the coming five years.[17]

What led the president to make such dramatic proposals? Several factors explain these initiatives. First, there was an increasing awareness in Congress and among the American public of the extraordinary scope and impact of the global human disaster resulting from HIV/AIDS, especially in Africa. It is estimated that 33 million people were living with HIV/AIDS in 2006, with 2 million deaths from the disease (see table 2-2). Deaths from AIDS per year are now double the number of deaths from malaria. And new infections continued to outpace the ability of the governments of affected countries and the international community to provide care and treatment: in 2005, for every new person receiving antiretroviral drugs, seven more were infected.[18] Further, HIV/AIDS was increasingly a disease

TABLE 2-2. Global Summary of the AIDS Epidemic, December 2007[a]

Number of people living with HIV in 2007

Total	33.2 million
	(30.6–36.1 million)
Adults	30.8 million
	(28.2–33.6 million)
Women	15.4 million
	(13.9–16.6 million)
Children younger than 15	2.5 million
	(2.2–2.6 million)

People newly infected with HIV in 2007

Total	2.5 million
	(1.8–4.1 million)
Adults	2.1 million
	(1.4–3.6 million)
Children younger than 15	420,000
	(350,000–540,000)

AIDS deaths in 2007

Total	2.1 million
	(1.9–2.4 million)
Adults	1.7 million
	(1.6–2.1 million)
Children younger than 15	330,000
	(310,000–380,000)

Source: UNAIDS and World Health Organization, *Epidemic Update 2007* (http://data.UNAIDS.org [January 2008]).
a. Numbers in parentheses indicate the possible range.

affecting women. Sixty percent of those with the disease were women and girls, and especially young girls—for each boy with the disease between the ages of fifteen and nineteen, there were seven infected girls.

As these facts became widely known, there was growing support among a variety of groups across the U.S. political spectrum—from gay activists and those concerned with the impact of the plague in Africa on the left to the religious right. For example, Rick Warren, pastor of one of the largest evangelical megachurches in the United States (Saddleback Church in Orange County, California, with 20,000 members), increasingly viewed the disease as afflicting innocents—especially women and children—and considered it a Christian duty to help. Thus, the president was able to make a series of dramatic and popular proposals on aid for fighting

BOX 2-1. U.S. Government Agencies Engaged in Fighting HIV/AIDS

President's Emergency Plan for AIDS Response (PEPFAR)
Department of State
U.S. Agency for International Development
Department of Health and Human Services
Department of Commerce
Department of Defense
Department of Labor
Peace Corps

HIV/AIDS, which would have bipartisan support and provide him with an important legacy.

Congress passed the United States Leadership against HIV/AIDS, Tuberculosis and Malaria Act in 2003, authorizing PEPFAR. After some internal competition between the Department of Health and Human Services and the Department of State for control of PEPFAR, it was decided to locate a global AIDS coordinator in the Department of State to manage the new program and to "oversee and direct" HIV/AIDS operations of all U.S. government agencies.

The first PEPFAR coordinator was Randall Tobias, former CEO of Eli Lilly and AT&T. He created a programming process and established several interagency committees to coordinate U.S. government AIDS policies. These included a policy group for principals, a deputy principals group that focuses on program management, a technical working group, country core teams, and a scientific steering committee. Within U.S. embassies in the field, the ambassador was charged with creating a team to draft five-year strategic plans and one-year operational plans to fight HIV/AIDS. Implementation of the PEPFAR funds fell to a considerable extent to USAID.

The principal activities to be funded with the new HIV/AIDS monies were prevention, treatment, and care. Congress earmarked 20 percent of the new funding for prevention, emphasizing abstinence before marriage, being faithful within marriage, and condom use (ABC), with at least one-third of prevention monies to go for activities encouraging abstinence and faithfulness. This earmark, together with a prohibition on providing PEPFAR assistance to any group "that does not have a policy explicitly opposing prostitution and sex trafficking," reflected the views and values of the Christian groups supporting the legislation but proved highly controversial with other constituencies involved in HIV/AIDS work. Responding to criticisms from the medical community and others of the abstinence earmark in particular, both the House and Senate passed legislation waiving the earmark on PEPFAR aid for abstinence in the aid appropriations bill for 2008.

Treatment provided antiretrovirals (ARVs) to those infected with the disease and care included programs for the rising numbers of AIDS orphans and vulnerable children. ARVs initially had to be brand-name drugs—that is, more expensive than generic drugs and thus likely to come from the large U.S. pharmaceutical companies. This provision was controversial and later relaxed to permit generic drug purchase if the drugs had been approved by the U.S. Food and Drug Administration. Fifteen "focus countries" were chosen (thirteen of which were in sub-Saharan Africa) for two-thirds of the new funding. U.S.-financed HIV/AIDS programs already existed in 100 countries worldwide; these countries would receive $4 billion in new funds. The final $1 billion would go the Global Fund to Fight AIDS, Tuberculosis, and Malaria.

In keeping with the management approach of the Bush administration (and the Clinton administration before it), PEPFAR would be accountable for achieving measurable results. Three goals were identified: (1) the prevention of 7 million new infections; (2) the treatment of 2 million infected people; and (3) care for 10 million of those infected or affected by the disease. Implementation programs in recipient countries would be based on the "three ones": one national plan; one national coordinating authority; and one national monitoring and evaluation system. Further, U.S.-funded programs should be tailored to local needs and conditions. There was, of course, a contradiction in these requirements: earmarks demanded that a portion of PEPFAR monies be spent for a particular purpose—prevention and abstinence—which collided with the goal of tailoring PEPFAR programs to local needs, conditions, and preferences.[19]

As of 2007, the overall performance of PEPFAR in getting up and running and making progress in achieving its goals had been impressive. By

F I G U R E   2 - 1. **Number of Individuals Receiving Antiretroviral Treatment**[a]

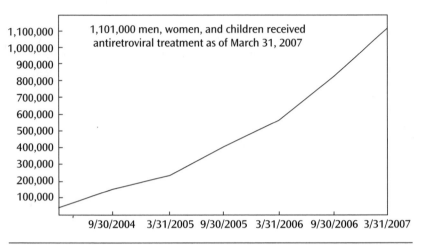

Source: President's Emergency Plan for AIDS Relief (PEPFAR) (http://www.pepfar.gov/press/85520.htm).
a. Total of both upstream and downstream U.S. government–supported interventions.

then, PEPFAR reported providing over 1 million people with ARVs and had proven that the delivery of significant amounts of funding and medicines was possible under the program (figure 2-1).

Additionally, 61 million people had been reached by PEPFAR-funded prevention campaigns, and the United States was supporting 2 million orphans and vulnerable children and providing care to another 2.4 million people living with HIV/AIDS. The program had proven that aid could be delivered effectively and affordably to large numbers of people—something that had been questioned by many, including senior U.S. officials, before the program began operations. What was not clear was exactly how many recipients of ARVs were supported directly by PEPFAR funding as well as how the recipients of ARVs were handling the drugs, whether the supply chains were reliable, and whether the many people reached with PEPFAR's prevention efforts actually changed their risky behavior. Finally, PEPFAR continued to enjoy bipartisan support, and prominent members of Congress from both political parties expressed their support for its reauthorization due in 2008 and appropriated an increase in HIV/AIDS funding for fiscal 2007 and 2008—in fact, more than the president requested. PEPFAR officials were optimistic about the program being reauthorized by Congress in 2008 and about the doubling in PEPFAR funding.

However, an evaluation by the Institute of Medicine (IOM) of the National Academy of Sciences, while praising the accomplishments thus far of PEPFAR, urged that several important amendments be made in the functioning of the program. One, mentioned above, was that the congressional earmarks on the funds be eliminated. Prevention programs including abstinence were critical to the fight against HIV/AIDS, but all prevention programs should be flexible enough to meet local cultural norms and conditions, harmonize with local plans, and not have their operations restricted by Washington. Second, the evaluation of the results of PEPFAR's activities should be based more on "outcomes" (that is, its impact on beneficiaries' lives and behavior and the evolution of the disease) and less on "outputs"—that is, how many people were reached by prevention campaigns or treatment and care.

Finally, a third and very important recommendation of the IOM evaluation was that PEPFAR should begin to transition from an emergency response entity focused on fighting HIV/AIDS to a sustainable program that would create the capabilities and conditions in afflicted countries so that those countries could sustain the fight against HIV/AIDS themselves. This recommendation is based on the reality that it is difficult to address chronic social problems effectively in isolation. In the case of HIV/AIDS, the fight cannot be sustained and won without stronger health systems, a larger number of trained health workers, and special provisions to protect vulnerable women and young girls. Most ambitiously, perhaps, is to improve the status of women through more education, reform of legal systems, and greater access to resources for women. Some of these functions were not permitted in PEPFAR's legislation. Ironically, the large amounts of HIV/AIDS funding were weakening the ability of health systems in poor countries to deal with other illnesses as personnel increasingly turned to work on care for AIDS patients.

PEPFAR, it was beginning to be argued, should take on the broader issues of development and social change that must be addressed if prevention, treatment, and care are to be effective and durable over the long term. Another reason for broadening the range of problems HIV/AIDS monies should address was the limitations on the capacity of local governments and organizations to use the sudden large increase in funding effectively—USAID officials in the field, who managed much of the PEPFAR monies, were already raising this problem quietly with headquarters in Washington and worried how they would be able to handle a doubling in five years. There were signs that PEPFAR was beginning to grapple with these issues to the extent that its authorizing legislation permitted it, including capacity building in health systems in recipient countries. But it was also evident that aid from other U.S. government programs was beginning to be directed to fund activities associated with the fight against HIV/AIDS, such as funding for nutritional supplements for those taking ARVs, reflecting the gravitational pull of the very large volume of aid tied to preventing, treating and caring for HIV/AIDS victims. The fact that one social problem, no matter how grave, is almost always linked to many others in what is often a seamless web has long been one of the basic challenges of development and is a challenge to effective fighting of HIV/AIDS.

There was also the worry among experts and observers that as the United States began to deliver ARVs to a growing number of individuals, it was taking on a long-term commitment to continue that support since it seemed unlikely that the poor in Africa and Asia or their governments would be able to finance their own medications in the foreseeable future. And, it should be remembered, the United States, along with other governments at the G-8 Summit at Gleneagles, at the UN High Level Meeting on HIV/AIDS in 2006, and elsewhere committed to helping all victims of HIV/AIDS gain access to ARVs by 2010—implying much larger commitments in the future. The United Nations estimates that to provide ARVs to all who need them would require over $22 billion a year. The provision of such a large amount of U.S. aid for HIV/AIDS and in particular for ARVs raised an issue unlike any other faced by U.S. foreign aid programs. Aid was keeping people alive through the antiviral drugs, but because so many were poor, and their governments were poor, they were unable to afford the drugs in the absence of aid. Should the U.S. government for any reason (funding fatigue, other more pressing priorities, such as budget constraints) decide to substantially reduce or terminate the funding with no other source of funding to replace it, the United States would be complicit in the certain deaths of those whose lives had been initially saved. This would be an ethically repugnant act for the U.S. government to commit. Thus, increasing funding for HIV/AIDS, above all for life-saving drugs, raises difficult questions about the long-term nature of U.S. aid, a topic to which I shall return in the next chapter.

USAID and "Transformational Diplomacy"

In his second inaugural speech in January 2005 President Bush declared, "The survival of liberty in our land increasingly depends on the success of liberty in other lands. . . . America's vital interests and our deepest beliefs are now one. . . . Across the generations we have proclaimed the imperative of self-government. . . . Now it is the urgent requirement of our nation's security, and the calling of our time. . . . So it is the policy of the United States to seek and support the growth of democratic movements and institutions in every nation and culture, with the ultimate goal of ending tyranny in our world."

These words promised a grand and ambitious global mission for the United States. Secretary of State Condoleezza Rice sought to turn the words into policy in her speech at Georgetown University almost a year later where she announced, "To achieve this bold mission, America needs equally bold diplomacy, a diplomacy that not only reports about the world as it is, but seeks to change the world itself. I and others have called this 'transformational diplomacy.'" The specific goal of transformational diplomacy was to "build and sustain democratic, well-governed states that will respond to the needs of their people and conduct themselves responsibly in the international system." In a speech at the State Department the following day, Secretary Rice declared that "foreign assistance is an essential component of our transformational diplomacy . . . to empower developing countries to strengthen security, to consolidate democracy, to increase trade and investment, and to improve the lives of their people . . . and to prevent future failed states like Afghanistan."

She announced that the USAID administrator would be "dual-hatted," becoming the director of U.S. foreign assistance (DFA), a new position that would have the rank of a deputy secretary of state and report directly to her. This person would be charged with better aligning foreign assistance with foreign policy goals and would have authority over all USAID programs (Development Assistance, Child Survival/Global Health, and PL480 food aid) and Department of State foreign assistance accounts, including PEPFAR, Economic Support Funds, Migration and Refugee Affairs, Andean Drug programs, and funding for projects and programs in Eastern Europe and the former Soviet Union. The director also had "coordinating authority" over other U.S. aid programs—the MCC and the numerous smaller aid programs located in some twenty-four federal departments and agencies. The reform was intended to rationalize and to bring greater coherence, transparency, and effectiveness to an increasingly fragmented system of aid within the U.S. government in support of transformational diplomacy. And it was also expected that a more transparent and rational aid system would help persuade Congress to make better informed decisions on the allocation and use of aid, and presumably to reduce the number of earmarks and directives that increasingly constrained much of the aid program.

Ambassador Randall Tobias was named the new U.S. director for foreign assistance, leaving his position as coordinator for PEPFAR. The director's office was created in April 2006 and physically located in the Department of State building. Called "F" for foreign assistance—elements of the Department of State reporting to the secretary typically have a single letter as their principal designation—the office eventually included roughly sixty staff from the USAID policy and budget office and from various State Department bureaus. F promptly set to work by creating an elaborate planning and programming process for the aid programs over which it had direct authority. This process came to be called the "F process." Specifically, Director Tobias listed four goals of the reforms:

◆ First, establishing a common foreign assistance strategy, and focusing our resources on the attainment of the goal and objectives of that strategy.

◆ Second, integrating our planning, budgeting, programming, and results reporting, at every level, so that we will always be able to

BOX 2-2. Strategic Framework: Country Categories

- *rebuilding countries* (states in or emerging from conflict)
- *developing countries* (low- or middle-income countries not eligible for MCC funds)
- *transforming countries* (low- or lower-middle-income countries eligible for MCC funding and meeting standards relating to political rights)
- *sustaining partner countries* (upper-middle-income countries)
- *restrictive countries* (states "of concern"—often with serious governance problems or with legislative restrictions prohibiting direct assistance or both)
- *regional programs* (programs that include more than one country)

make decisions on the basis of a full and coordinated picture of how our resources will work together.

- Third, improving the transparency of all that we do in connection with our foreign assistance resources.
- Strengthening accountability for the results that are—or are not—achieved with these resources.[20]

In structuring the reforms, Tobias and his planning team took a very logical approach, much as was done in setting up PEPFAR earlier. First, they identified five broad objectives for foreign aid:

- Creating peace and security
- Supporting just and democratic governance
- Encouraging investment in people
- Supporting economic growth
- Providing humanitarian assistance

They then created a strategic framework to categorize developing countries and the types of aid they would receive. This framework was drawn from an earlier analysis in a USAID white paper, *U.S. Foreign Aid: Meeting the Challenges of the Twenty First Century* (2004).[21]

The strategic framework included categories "based on common traits, and places them on a trajectory of progress, with the ultimate intent of supporting recipient country efforts to move from a relationship defined by dependence on traditional foreign assistance to one defined by full sustaining partnership status."[22] To strengthen the framework on which this process would be based and to provide more information on how aid funds from all sources were used, a detailed classification of the activities funded by aid was also developed—some 407 objectives, program areas, elements, and subelements—to be applied to all U.S. aid expenditures. Part of the goal in collecting these data was to give government officials, members of Congress, their staffs, and the public detailed data on how much money the United States spends on particular types of activities and where it is spent—information that had not been collected in such detail previously (see box 2-3). Secretary Rice reportedly once asked her staff how much the United States was spending on democracy promotion, but no one was able to give her an answer—a story (whether true or not) often told to explain why the F process required so much data.

Within the State-USAID mission strategic plans developed for individual countries, each USAID operating unit (that is, field mission and central offices in Washington) would submit an annual operational plan showing how funds would be spent to achieve the goals of transformational diplomacy and, it was hoped, move the country from one development category to the next. Country working groups in Washington would use these plans to determine the overall aid budget for individual recipient countries and, to a considerable extent, how the funds would be spent.

Finally, Tobias reportedly planned to rationalize the use of U.S. aid by assigning specific activities to particular agencies, thus cutting down on duplication, for example, between what the Department of State did and what USAID did in their two separate democracy promotion programs.[23]

Many of the goals and procedures of the F process made a great deal of sense and were long overdue. Better data on aid expenditures from all sources were essential to effective programming, budgeting, and transparency. A strategic planning process that began with an overall foreign policy goal and then derived country programs and budgets to support that goal was reasonable. It also made sense to align the way U.S. aid was spent with the characteristics of particular recipient countries rather than to develop budgets on the basis of sector accounts (for example, health, family planning) with amounts dictated from Washington as had been the dominant approach in the past.

However, the implementation of the F process reforms came to be seen as increasingly problematical by many in USAID, State, Congress, and among NGOs and contractors, the latter two being important constituents

BOX 2-3. The "F process" and Enabling Evidence-Based Dialogue: A Perspective from the Inside

Within the U.S. government, over 20 departments and agencies operate their own foreign assistance programs. They use different methodologies for accounting and performance evaluation. The result is a myriad of databases collecting inconsistent and incomparable data. The absence of a common system limits our ability to consistently compare the performance of one program to another, of one implementing partner to another, or of one recipient country to another. Without a common framework, we are left with anecdotes only for learning and application of best practices.

Twenty-first-century technology allows us to systematically collect and analyze detailed information across borders with more efficiency and precision than ever before. The Office of the Director of U.S. Foreign Assistance (F) was established to better coordinate and rationalize the many foreign assistance programs implemented by the U.S. government. F sought to enhance the accountability, effectiveness, efficiency, and credibility of foreign assistance by introducing a system of coordinated planning, budgeting, and evaluation that would answer three principal questions:

◆ How are foreign assistance funds being used?
◆ What is being achieved with these funds?
◆ Are these outcomes the right outcomes for both U.S. foreign policy goals and sustainable impact on poverty reduction?

To answer the three questions, F developed a uniform system to record, measure, and assess various types of U.S. government assistance programs across over 150 countries. Under the director of U.S. Foreign Assistance's guidance, State and USAID staff built a common set of program definitions and indicators with input from the nongovernmental organization (NGO) community. To ensure that all appropriate forms of assistance were captured by this system, definitions and indicators were posted online for review for a full year with an accompanying email address for comments and suggestions.

Additional contributions to the common data collection system included a State-USAID review of annual operational plans, a computer system that uniformly tracked budget allocations to specific activities by country, a computer system that captured and extracted information from the operational plans, and a revised congressional budget presentation that provided data on U.S. assistance by program, by country, and by objective.

The intention of these efforts was to collect information to enable evidence-based decisionmaking and dialogue between the numerous foreign assistance stakeholders. Over time, F staff hoped that one data collection system would allow the executive branch, Congress, NGOs, businesses, and international partners to move away from anecdote-based dialogue to engage in rigorous, thoughtful discussions about the intent, impact, and funding of U.S. foreign assistance. We hoped to improve the focus and effectiveness of U.S. government efforts toward the core goal of foreign assistance—helping people around the world to live in societies that allow them to reach their highest potential.

Laura Wilson
Former Senior Advisor to Ambassador Randall Tobias,
Director of U. S. Foreign Assistance and Administrator, USAID
U.S. Department of State

of U.S. aid, and its main implementers. There were two types of problems: the way the reforms were elaborated—that is, their substantive details— and the manner in which they were implemented.

Problems of Substance

There were five problems of substance or policy associated with the F reforms. One involved the goal that aid was supposed to advance—transformational diplomacy. A second involved the way aid was proposed to advance that goal—the strategic framework developed for programming aid. A third was the set of organizational issues raised by a partial integration of USAID and the Department of State. A fourth involved data and programming processes. And fifth was the impression that the F process represented a recentralization of decisionmaking in Washington from what had been a field-based organization with considerable authority delegated to field staff for programming and implementation.

First, the goal of transformational diplomacy had two fundamental elements: one was promoting development—"democratic, well-governed states that will respond to the needs of their people."[24] And the other was supporting U.S. diplomacy—encouraging states "to conduct themselves responsibly in the international system," presumably including supporting U.S. policies, especially the global war on terrorism. There appears to have been an assumption that these two goals were mutually reinforcing— that democratic, well-governed states would act responsibly from the U.S. point of view. But that was a leap of faith; U.S. policies were supported by countries that were not democratic or responsive to the needs of their peoples. Pakistan comes to mind as an important example. And other countries were democratic but did not support many U.S. policies. Would France perhaps at times fit into this category? Venezuela? Egypt if it actually had free and fair elections? Many countries fit somewhat into both of these categories, and others moved back and forth.

At another level, democracy, development, and responsible behavior were apparently seen as linked: democratic states were more peaceable— an assumption made by both the Bush and Clinton administrations. It was thought that they enjoyed peace and security at home because they were legitimate in the eyes of their citizens, who had a voice in policies and held governments accountable, and were more peaceable internationally— "behaved responsibly"—since they did not go to war with other democratic states.[25] Importantly, they did not—in theory—become failing or failed states and thus sources or sanctuaries for terrorists.

There would be little argument from most development experts that governance and institutional capacity were at the core of the most difficult development problems worldwide and often associated with state failure. But the understanding of basic causes and consequences of governance problems, which, lest we forget, can and do exist in established democracies, is still unsettled and often in dispute. And while there is a clear relationship between democracy and prosperity in the long run, it is far from clear that in the short or medium term democracy leads to improved governance. It is not proof against corruption and conflict— indeed, transitions from autocracy to democracy often intensify conflict.

The disconnect between democracy, development, and diplomacy is a basic flaw in the concept of transformational diplomacy. It obscures the very real tension, and sometimes conflict, that can exist between the requirements of development and the imperatives of diplomacy; and it can emerge in decisions on country allocation and use of aid.

A second problem with the substance of the F process was the strategic framework for aid giving (described above). If the framework had been simply a convenient classification of countries with no presumption that it was precise or that countries fit neatly into the separate categories or progressed naturally from one end (recovering from conflict) to the other (to democratic governance and economic prosperity), it might have been a useful conceptual tool. Further, neither the five goals nor the country categories included aid for primarily diplomatic relationships, which were an essential element in U.S. aid giving, undoubtedly fueling a fear within the Department of State that the F process represented a takeover by USAID of State's assistance programs.

As it turned out, the goals and country categories tended to be used as programming tools, turning them into an instrument of decisionmaking. As a result, the application of this framework produced budget and program results, which some in the development community, Congress, and the executive branch found difficult to understand. For example, Senator Patrick Leahy, chair of the Subcommittee on State, Foreign Operations, and Related Programs of the Senate Appropriations Committee, questioned cuts in aid to Nepal, just emerging from a Maoist conflict, and to the Democratic Republic of the Congo, strategically positioned in Africa and also (it was hoped) emerging from a long civil war. Plus, cuts in democracy promotion activities in Russia (barely hanging on to democracy) and others provoked considerable criticism from members of Congress.[26]

Third, there were organizational issues raised by the integration of budgets and planning by USAID and the Department of State in the creation of F. There was a general concern (shared by this author) that combining State and USAID budget processes would eventually lead to a takeover by State of USAID's assistance programs and the loss of that agency's development mission. This was not the intention of the F process reforms or of Secretary Rice or Director Tobias, but it was the fear in much of the development community inside and outside the government, especially with regard to what would happen after the current officials involved in the reforms were replaced by others with less interest in the rationalization of aid for development. Ironically, as mentioned above, many in the Department of State feared exactly the reverse was happening: that USAID and its development goals were absorbing State aid programs and the diplomatic purposes they served.

In the 2008 budget process, budget decisions reinforced the fear that USAID and its mission was being absorbed by State. First, funding requested for USAID's development assistance account (the primary source of development-oriented bilateral aid) was cut by one-third from the 2007 level, while the Economic Support Funds (ESF—controlled traditionally by the Department of State) rose by 25 percent. Second, funding for USAID's operating expenses that are essential to managing a complex aid program (USAID implements not just its Development Assistance and Global Health/Child Survival accounts but ESF, food aid, and a number of other aid accounts) were cut while operating expenses for the Department of State were increased.[27] These shifts were explained by Tobias in his testimonies to Congress in early 2007 as an effort to rationalize the current aid system. However, his explanation proved unconvincing and prompted Representative Nita Lowey, chair of the key Subcommittee on State, Foreign Operations, and Related Programs of the House Appropriations Committee, to complain that

I've seen a budget request which gutted the Development Assistance account and reallocated funding to an account with other priorities, which could lead to a shift in funding away from long-term development programs. And I have seen a budget request which sizably increases the operating costs of the State Department yet cuts funding for USAID's operating costs. . . . The result is that AID has become more of a procurement mechanism and less of a policy shop.[28]

These views were also voiced by InterAction, the umbrella organization that represents 165 development and relief NGOs, when it criticized the Bush administration for shortsightedness for giving the secretary of state "control over American foreign assistance," citing decisions made in the F process that appeared to downplay poverty concerns and support security objectives.[29] Other NGOs began to voice similar apprehensions. A remark by a Department of State spokesperson seemed to confirm these fears. When questioned about the notion of the reforms being a power grab on the part of the State Department, Sean McCormack remarked, "These shifts are designed to give ambassadors more flexibility."[30]

Further inflaming concerns in USAID and in Congress about the F process were plans on the part of Tobias to close a number of USAID missions in the field and appoint "development attachés" or rely on regional missions to manage aid activities in "transforming countries," those eligible for MCC funding. While this policy may have made sense as Tobias sought to rationalize the responsibilities of different U.S. aid agencies, it was seen as yet another move to shrink the presence and mission of USAID and to cut U.S. engagement in many countries where USAID had been present for decades. It was especially worrisome since little of the MCC's funding had actually been disbursed to its eligible recipients.

The fourth problem with the substance of the F reforms was the amount of detail demanded in the F process data and programming requirements. Producing useful data was an important element in the reform process, but the amount of information required from USAID missions on their proposed expenditures was very large and proved extremely time consuming to collect. Further, the country operational plans required of USAID missions reportedly reached hundreds of pages each—far larger than busy officials or congressional staffers had time to read or analyze.[31]

Fifth, during this early stage of the F process, it looked very much like what had in the past been a relatively decentralized programming and implementation system in USAID, with considerable decisionmaking power delegated to field missions, was being centralized in Washington. "Strategy" decisions now made at headquarters were interpreted broadly, with limited input from the field (and limited information on the process transmitted to the field). This trend provoked criticisms by USAID staff, and eventually staff and members of Congress, that programming and budgetary decisions were less transparent than at any time in the past.

These five problems fed growing unease on the part of USAID professionals, staff and members of Congress, and in the development community regarding the direction of the reforms. But it was the style of their implementation that turned unease into alarm and resistance on the part of many.

Problems of Style

An additional set of problems arose in the way the F process was implemented. First, the key decisionmakers were Tobias and a small inner circle of staff. While many of the staff were exceedingly able, some lacked experience in the bureaucracy and in the politics of aid in Washington. They were seen as closed and overly protective of Tobias, but they were apparently reflecting his preferred operating style. And they were mostly young—causing some resentment among more senior officials in USAID and State to whom they were giving directions.

Second, decisions involving the changes in the F process were made in ways perceived as preemptory and autocratic by USAID and State officials and others outside the administration, causing further resentment and resistance. Third, old policies were discarded with relatively little discussion within the bureaucracy with those who were going to have to implement the new policies. There was almost no preparation of the bureaucracy and others for the large scope and rapid implementation of the reforms. This rushed process produced confusion and feelings of disempowerment by experienced professionals, adding to problems of morale and criticisms of the changes. Further, the fact that the director spent nearly all his time in the Department of State rather than at his

USAID office also sent a signal to USAID staff, whether accurate or not, that he was uninterested in their views or their work.

There were extensive briefings inside and outside government on the content of the reforms. While these were sometimes described as "consultations," they were seen by many as involving more the delivery of information than a listening to concerns and an exchange of views.[32] The perceived lack of consultations with Congress and the apparent direction of the reform process provoked sharp critiques from members of the House and Senate, including Representative Tom Lantos, then chair of the House Foreign Affairs Committee, Senator Patrick Leahy, chair of the Subcommittee on State, Foreign Operations, and Related Programs of the Senate Appropriations Committee, and from Senator Robert Menendez, member of the Senate Foreign Relations Committee. Menendez echoed the others on the reform process when he complained that

> The foreign aid reform process was carried out in an exclusive, secretive manner. People refer to the "F process" as a black box without any real input or consultation, except for post-facto briefings, with Congress, with the NGO community, or others inside the government.
>
> The process was top-down and excluded valuable input from the people in the field who know the most about what is happening on the ground. . . .
>
> USAID is in the process of being decimated as its funding, role, and mission are reduced.[33]

Randall Tobias resigned on April 27, 2007, after he admitted using a Washington escort service, and just a year after he had taken on the job. Even without Tobias's sudden departure, the rising chorus of criticism of the F process made it seem likely that the process, and Tobias himself, were headed for trouble, especially with Congress. Some of the processes put in place under his leadership have remained, some have been adjusted, and others appear to be in limbo.[34] Tobias's successor, Henrietta Fore, former undersecretary of state for management, has taken steps to reach out to the NGO community, listen to senior USAID management, incorporate the field perspective, simplify the budget and planning process, and reduce Washington involvement in implementation, leaving the basic principles of the reform in place. However, it seems that the reform process will remain in a holding pattern, with some adjustments, for the remainder of the Bush administration.

Department of Defense

Every three years or so, the Development Assistance Committee of the Organization for Economic Cooperation and Development (OECD) produces an in-depth study of the foreign economic assistance programs of each member state (including most aid-giving countries of Europe, North America, and Japan) and the European Union. The most recent of these studies of U.S. aid offered a statistic that surprised many: in 2005, 22 percent of U.S. official development assistance was provided by the Department of Defense (DoD), up from 3.5 percent in 1998 and second only to USAID, which provided 39 percent.[35] Much of DoD's aid was provided for reconstruction in Iraq and Afghanistan, where U.S. troops are operating in often very insecure environments. But there have been policy changes in DoD that suggested that the Pentagon is moving into the aid-giving business in a significant and sustained way, and not only in countries where the United States is engaged in military operations.

DoD's mission has been expanded to include activities falling into the traditional domain of development. Defense Department Directive 3000.05 stated that "Stability operations are a core U.S. military mission that the Department of Defense shall be prepared to conduct and support. They shall be given priority comparable to combat operations and be explicitly addressed and integrated across all DoD activities. . . . Stability operations are conducted to help establish order that advances U.S. interests and values. The immediate goal often is to provide the local populace with security, restore essential services, and meet humanitarian needs. The long-term goal is to help develop indigenous capacity for securing essential services, a viable market economy, rule of law, democratic institutions and a robust civil society."[36]

The Quadrennial Defense Review for 2006–09 (an overall national defense strategy and planning document) reiterated the requirement that the U.S. military "must be trained, ready to operate and able to make decisions in traditionally non-military areas, such as disaster response and stabilization."[37]

In 2006, in response to active lobbying by DoD, the National Defense Authorization Act (section 1206) allowed the Department of Defense "to spend up to $200 million of its own appropriations to train and equip foreign militaries to undertake counterterrorism or stability operations." This language in effect provided the Pentagon with the ability to create its own military assistance program (the existing military assistance budget had been housed in the Department of State to ensure the assistance was used in concert with U.S. diplomacy in recipient countries). DoD has recently proposed to amend section 1206 to include a "Building Global Partnership Act" that would give DoD permanent and global authorities to provide assistance directly (including humanitarian and stabilization aid) anywhere U.S. troops are operating rather than have to obtain the concurrence of the secretary of state. Congress has been reluctant to agree to all of these proposals but supported a three-year pilot phase to test DoD's ideas, with some restrictions on where the funds could be spent and requirements that Defense coordinate with the Department of State and the director of U.S. Foreign Assistance.[38]

The Commanders' Emergency Response Program (CERP) enables military commanders to distribute funds to assist communities where they are operating. It is estimated that up to 2007, DoD spent roughly $2 billion of CERP funds in Iraq, in addition to funds disbursed by the Department of State, USAID, and other U.S. government agencies. The 2008 DoD budget has requested $1 billion in CERP funds with considerable flexibility as to where they would be spent worldwide.[39]

Provincial Reconstruction Teams (PRTs) have also been set up by Defense to provide assistance for reconstruction in Afghanistan and Iraq. These teams, led and to a considerable extent staffed by the U.S. military, have funded projects related to security and development in these countries. Goals for PRTs in Iraq include "bolstering moderates, promoting reconciliation, supporting counterinsurgency operations, fostering economic growth and developing capacity."[40]

The U.S. military—led by the U.S. Army—has created three major programs in sub-Saharan Africa: the Combined Joint Task Force–Horn of Africa, the East Africa Counterterrorism Initiative, and the Trans-Sahara Counterterrorism Initiative, each with funding not only to help train local military and security forces but to fund school construction, well digging, and other development-oriented activities.

The U.S. Navy has created an African Partnership Station in Naples to support a greater engagement of its personnel in West and Central African countries where its ships make port calls—a longer stay with possibly more frequent visits combined with an effort on the part of sailors to do a variety of good works (possibly partnering with NGOs like Project Hope) in these countries.[41]

On February 6, 2007, President Bush announced the creation of AFRICOM—a new unified military command to cover Africa. (Africa had previously been divided between the European, Central, and Pacific Commands.) This move, which will take several years to implement, signaled a much heightened interest on the part of the U.S. military in Africa. General Banz J. Craddock of the European Command has argued, "The large ungoverned area in Africa, HIV/AIDS epidemic, corruption, weak governance, and poverty that exist throughout the continent are challenges that are key factors in the security stability issues that affect every country in Africa."[42] It seemed clear that AFRICOM would become active in stability and development operations on the continent. It was described as "promoting a greater unity of effort across the government in Africa."[43] The deputy commander for civil-military affairs is a State Department officer.

There are several basic contradictions in what DoD says its intentions are, especially with regard to AFRICOM. Contradiction 1 is this: Officials say they want to address the problems leading to instability in Africa—poverty, weak state institutions, lack of democracy, and weak security services; they also say that they do not intend to run large assistance programs or duplicate what others are doing. However, the problems they propose to address are essentially development problems and are enormous, complicated, and expensive to address and require a long-term and well-informed commitment—they are the same problems that all development agencies face. Contradiction 2, with special regard to AFRICOM, is that Defense officials stress that they have no intention of taking over or compromising the functions of the Department of State, U.S. ambassadors in the field, or USAID in their stabilization work in Africa while also affirming that they intended to bring everyone together under AFRICOM's umbrella to coordinate stabilization policies (on a regional basis). If they are the conveners, they will shape and possibly drive the political agenda in their regions and potentially encroach on the authorities of U.S. ambassadors and the Department of State. In any case, it is difficult to align regional and country-focused policies, another mini-contradiction that may make the stated role of AFRICOM difficult to achieve. These contradictions are of particular concern to the Department of State, which understandably does not want to see the authorities of U.S. ambassadors in the field eroded or circumscribed by another U.S. agency.

What is behind these contradictions? My suspicion is that Defense officials have yet to sort out fully what is involved to achieve their stabilization objectives abroad and the implications of their initiatives for U.S. foreign policy. So what is driving these initiatives by DoD? There appear to be four major factors: (1) its new global war on terror mission to support stabilization in developing countries where ungoverned spaces, poverty, and discontent can produce or harbor terrorists; (2) a frustration over the lack of resources on the part of the civilian agencies to address stabilization issues adequately; (3) an effort to create a relationship for a military presence should that be needed in the future and to ensure friendly relations with communities in countries where there is a military presence; and (4) the natural tendency of bureaucracies to expand the scope of their activities (and their budgets) to fit their missions. The main factor appears to be frustration on the part of DoD in getting the stabilization job done quickly by civilian agencies. For example, Defense Secretary Robert Gates recently remarked that

One of the most important lessons from our experience in Iraq, Afghanistan, and elsewhere has been the decisive role reconstruction, development, and governance plays in any meaningful, long-term success.

The Department of Defense has taken on many of these burdens that might have been assumed by civilian agencies in the past . . . forced by circumstances, our brave men and women in uniform have stepped up to the task, with field artillerymen and tankers building schools and mentoring city councils—usually in a language they don't speak. They have done an admirable job. And as I've said before, the Armed Forces will need to institutionalize and retain these non-traditional capabilities—something the ROTC cadets in this audience can anticipate.

But it is no replacement for the real thing—civilian involvement and expertise.

What is clear to me is that there is a need for a dramatic increase in spending on the civilian instruments of national security—diplomacy, strategic communications, foreign assistance, civic action, and economic reconstruction and development."[44]

The comments by Gates were a statement of fact, a lamentation, a recommendation, and, whether intended or not, a threat that DoD would have to do the job of stabilization itself if civilian agencies lacked the resources, capacity, or will to do so.

The lead role of DoD in Iraq and its increasing role in stabilization operations—postconflict work, development, and nation building—undoubtedly helped spur the Department of State to create a rapid response capacity of its own to permit it to do much of the same things in postconflict situations: to provide relief, reconstruction, and help rebuild national institutions. In August 2004 the Department of State announced the creation of a Coordinator for Reconstruction and Stabilization (S/CRS). A number of reports by think tanks and others had earlier urged the creation of such a capacity in State. The mission of S/CRS as proposed is "to lead, coordinate and institutionalize U.S. Government civilian capacity to prevent or prepare for post-conflict situations, and to help stabilize and reconstruct societies in transition from conflict or civil strife, so they can reach a sustainable path toward peace, democracy and a market economy."[45] This new office would have a staff of more than thirty full-time experts with the hope of adding another fifty-seven (with nineteen of them full time) in 2008.[46] It will create a cadre of some 100 experts to be on stand-by as "first responders" in case of need abroad; and it would have a $100-million-a-year contingency Conflict Response Fund to use in case of need.

However, S/CRS has been slow to get up and running because of resistance inside the Department of State and skepticism in Congress. Congress was particularly dubious of a program based on contingencies—it rarely likes to appropriate monies for contingencies—and did not approve any funding, though DoD was permitted to transfer $100 million to the

Department of State to support S/CRS. But the new office has yet to live up to its potential.

The DoD initiatives listed above point to a much greater involvement on the part of the U.S. military in providing economic assistance. This function is not new to DoD. Since the Eisenhower administration, there have been "civic action" programs in various parts of the world—for example, Latin America, where the U.S. military helped local militaries assist development of countries there by building infrastructure. However, civic action programs got a bad name during the Vietnam war and were much reduced.[47] The need on the part of combatant commanders for resources to fund immediate reconstruction where U.S. troops are operating in highly insecure environments, like Iraq, is understandable. However, fighting terrorism provides a new rationale and impetus for the U.S. military providing economic assistance in noncombat zones.

But this mission creep (or mission leap) raises basic questions about whether it is sensible or effective for the military to provide aid in support of long-term development. One former military officer observed that "military culture is antithetical to the culture that's needed for long-term development. Development of civil society is about ambiguities, gray areas, embracing debate and consensus and questioning authority. . . . Those are not the things a military does well."[48] Further, DoD lacks the programming processes and professional staff to manage an effective development aid program. A school building project or a well provided to villages may be a nice public relations move, but it does little to contribute to a region's or country's overall development and is often abandoned and forgotten unless part of a broader development strategy, implemented over the long term and "owned" by the intended beneficiaries.

DoD's entry into the long-term development field has also raised concerns among development specialists inside and outside the U.S. government. They fear that U.S. economic assistance may be perceived abroad as becoming militarized, which could prove dangerous for those delivering it and lead to its rejection by its intended beneficiaries. And it adds yet another potentially major player in the already cluttered policy and organizational landscape of aid giving within the U.S. government. Despite these hesitations, the trend of DoD's engaging in aid giving seems to be progressing inexorably, implicit in its role in responding to terrorist threats.

Summing Up

The changes in U.S. foreign aid during the Bush administration—above all the increases in aid, the creation of two important new agencies (MCC, PEPFAR), the expansion of DoD's role as a development actor, and the partial integration of USAID and State—are of major significance. Taken together, they have begun to transform the face of American assistance. But they also raise two sets of problems. First, in each case, the idea behind the initiatives was worthy, but the implementation was flawed. The worst case of this is the F process reforms, which were implemented so poorly that they caused considerable disruption and demoralization within USAID and growing criticism from Congress and outside groups. Many of the reforms have been halted or abandoned since the departure of Tobias.

The MCC, despite the Bush administration's commitments that it would produce much more effective aid programs in a few years, has been slow to get up and running and has yet to realize its promise. As a result, Congress has refused to appropriate the full amounts requested by the administration and has become increasingly critical of its operations. PEPFAR has made an excellent start on realizing its promise, but the very size of its aid and its narrow focus on fighting one disease have raised questions about its impact on development overall in recipient countries and whether its programs are sustainable—especially compelling in this case because human lives depend on its funding.

Finally, and perhaps most problematical, is the rise of the Department of Defense in the aid-giving business. What will be the extent and limitations on its activities in this area? These questions have yet to be answered, even by DoD. The obvious pattern here is one of good ideas but limited or flawed implementation—a pattern not uncommon in other policies of the Bush administration.

But in addition to the complications involving each of these initiatives, they raise one more question: how do they fit together? The truth is that they do not. The rhetoric of elevating development—which is a multifaceted undertaking—seems inconsistent with the reality of putting an enormous volume of aid into addressing one element of that undertaking, health and HIV/AIDS in particular. Defense's increasing role could challenge the professionalism and impact of the overall U.S. development effort. The endeavor to impart greater coherence to all development aid through the F process reforms has failed, and together with the creation of the MCC and PEPFAR and the Defense efforts, these reforms have left U.S. aid more fragmented and less coherent than ever. Underlying this basic problem is that these programs were conceived separately with little common planning and absent an overall vision of how the United States could elevate development in U.S. foreign policy and support it effectively abroad. In short, the administration made a good start on producing a transformation in foreign aid and, at the same time, has also exacerbated the chaos in U.S. aid-giving.

THREE

Outstanding Policy Issues

Each of the initiatives described in the previous chapter raises important and unresolved policy issues with regard to the allocation and use of U.S. foreign aid. Some of these issues have already been touched on. This chapter examines in depth several of the more prominent ones not fully examined in chapter 2.

The Millenium Challenge Corporation: Demonstrating More Effective Aid

Aid for development has alternated between an emphasis on promoting growth—through economic reforms, infrastructure expansion, business service centers to provide advice and training for entrepreneurs, and enterprise funds to provide credit to small, medium-size, and midmarket enterprises—and addressing problems of poverty directly, for example, by expanding basic health and education, microenterprise lending, and community development.[1] The 1960s put primary emphasis on fostering growth by creating the conditions that would foster expanded private investment and increased productivity in existing enterprises; the 1970s focused directly on meeting the basic human needs of the poor, such as by expanding basic education, health care, and rural, small farmer development; the 1980s saw a return to growth as a priority through policy reform; and poverty reduction was the theme of the 1990s.

The Millenium Challenge Corporation (MCC) represents a reemphasis on growth by assisting countries whose policies are already deemed relatively good for promoting growth based on eighteen criteria. The MCC monies are also intended to create an incentive for other governments with less adequate policies to implement economic and political reforms and to boost their growth prospects and thus their eligibility for MCC funding.

The core idea behind the MCC is that good policies will result in effective development and poverty reduction and that those policies can be identified and countries classified according to good policy performance. This seems an eminently logical assumption. Poor policies—large-scale corruption, repression and insecurity, hyperinflation, grossly misaligned exchange rates, major barriers to trade and investment—will surely discourage investment, possibly lead to political turmoil and civil conflict, and block sustained growth and development in the future as they have done in the past, for example, in the Democratic Republic of the Congo, Haiti, Sierra Leone, Burma, and elsewhere. But this paradigm rests on several key assumptions that remain to be tested.

First, it is assumed that countries can easily be assessed by using objective measures of "good" and "bad" policies and that those policies are sufficiently influential so as to have a predictable impact on their growth. In fact, many countries have a mix of good and bad policies and have nevertheless been able to enjoy rapid growth. China is the most prominent example of a country with corruption, weak rule of law, and a host of other problems but that has been growing at an incredible rate since the 1980s. Indonesia is another with a history of extensive corruption and healthy growth. It seems likely that other factors besides those captured by the eighteen indicators matter, too, for example, population size. Even with all its problems, China is too big a market and too low cost a producer for hungry investors to ignore if there is a shred of possibility they might be able to make money investing there.

The same is clearly not true for many African countries. Paul Collier notes in his excellent book that small, landlocked, natural-resource-rich or conflict-ridden countries tend to have a much harder time developing, and using aid effectively to spur growth, than countries without these problems.[2] The right policies are important, but they may not be enough.

This may be why some data-based studies have found no relationship between aid effectiveness and policies of the recipient country.[3] With the complexities of the multiple factors, alone or in combination, spurring growth, the MCC is more of an experiment in improving aid effectiveness than an exercise with predictable results, despite the fact that it has been presented to Congress and the public as the latter.

In addition to the very difficult challenge of demonstrating cause and effect between aid and growth, there is another important question facing the MCC: how much aid is really needed in order to have a significant impact in a country? We do not yet have enough information to try to answer that question since the amounts of aid provided through the MCC thus far have turned out to be much smaller than originally envisioned and so are likely in most cases to make a relatively small contribution to the availability of resources to recipient governments. For example, as of July 2007, if we compare the average annual commitments of aid in signed MCC country compacts with total aid disbursed from all sources in 2005 (the latest data from the Development Assistance Committee) in those countries, MCC flows (had all commitments actually been disbursed) would have averaged less than 15 percent of total aid flows that year, with a very large increase in aid flows (by 250 percent) only in Lesotho. These are very rough guidelines to the potential addition in aid represented by the MCC since (1) very little of the MCC monies have in fact been disbursed; (2) they are planned for disbursement in gradually increasing levels over time; and (3) by the time they are actually disbursed (2008–12), aid flows from other sources to MCC countries may have risen significantly from the level in 2005. These percentages do raise the question as to whether MCC aid, once it begins to be spent, will be large enough to have the impact intended on a recipient country's growth. Again, the MCC is a worthy trial, but it is not an exercise in applying known technologies to promote major economic change in foreign lands.

The MCC also was intended to have an effect on countries not eligible for receiving its funds—the promise of sizeable amounts of aid was supposed to provide incentives for governments to undertake the reforms to make them eligible for MCC funding and to sustain those reforms over time. In addition, the MCC was meant to spur recipient countries to undertake further reforms—for example in procurement practices—to meet MCC standards of operations. Has it had those effects? A 2006 study by two Harvard economists suggests such an "MCC incentive effect" exists.[4] If confirmed by additional studies, this could be an important achievement for the MCC. However, it must begin to disburse more aid, in much larger amounts, to sustain any such effect.

Another issue in MCC programming is the assumption that low-income recipient countries would be able to muster the capacity to propose their own MCC-funded aid activities and to manage those activities effectively. It is well known that poor countries typically have weak governmental capacities, no matter how good their policies are. But the slowness with which the MCC has been able to disburse its funds in the field—part but not all of which is a result of MCC's own start-up problems—raises the question whether those capacities are too limited to handle MCC requirements in a reasonable time period, even with technical assistance from the MCC. If, upon careful analysis, this proves to be the case, the MCC model may have to be fundamentally revised to take into account the capacity problem in low-income recipient countries and the implications of that problem for implementation and rates of disbursement.

Finally, there is the challenge of demonstrating to Congress and the American public that MCC funding is effective in promoting growth and poverty reduction in recipient countries—the claim that helped gain congressional support for this new type of aid agency. There are two parts to this challenge. One, mentioned above, is familiar: demonstrating the connection between the aid and its impact. This in itself is a difficult challenge; but in addition, the political clock is running: MCC legislation is to be reauthorized in 2008 when its impact will inevitably be a topic of discussion. At the current rate of disbursements, it will be very hard to demonstrate its impact or even to achieve expected outputs.

The second part of the challenge involves a question seldom asked but nonetheless very important: How much aid effectiveness is enough? Naturally, there is an expectation that aid should achieve its goals—for example, that roads are built to specification and are maintained; that agricultural production and sales increase as foreseen; and that farmers' incomes grow by the expected amount. But things seldom turn out as intended. Local conditions can present unexpected problems; designated technologies may not work as planned in a new environment; management of aid interventions can be ineffective on donor and recipient sides; unintended side effects of an aid intervention or events beyond the control of donor or recipient can undercut the impact of the aid. Of course, it is also possible for unexpected events to strengthen rather than undo the impact of an aid-funded activity. In short, attempting to bring about beneficial change in foreign countries is a risky and often experimental business. Where aid evaluators report consistently 100 percent effectiveness, they are probably gaming the system or not taking enough risks for change. So what should we expect regarding successes and failures of aid projects and programs? For example, should we laud or lament a 70 percent rate of achieving intended outcomes?

There is no accepted benchmark, but one way of getting at an answer to this question is to look at similarly risky investments in the private sector. For example, what degree of success do early stage venture capitalists expect from their risk capital? They face the same uncertainties regarding new technologies, the quality of managers implementing projects, and the economic environment in which the project is undertaken. Apparently, venture capitalists do not like to advertise their rates of success or failure, but from several sources it appears that the following pattern is common: roughly 25–30 percent fail, 40–50 percent break even or have moderate success, and 10–20 percent attain outstanding success (where success is measured in rates of return on investment).[5]

How does this stack up against what we know of past aid successes and failures? Bearing in mind that this is the crudest of comparisons and can only be taken so far, there appear to have been fewer transformational successes in aid—the high-yielding varieties of grain could certainly be counted as one of them. There also appear to have been fewer clear failures. For example, the World Bank estimated that between 1974 and 1994, 72 percent of its projects were rated "satisfactory." In 1995 that percentage fell slightly to 68 percent but rose to 78 percent by 2000.[6] The U.K. Department for International Development found that its aid projects achieved their purpose (meaning "outputs") an average of 62 percent of the time in 1986–89, rising to 78 percent in 1994–99. The goals (more like "outcomes" in this study) of British aid projects were achieved at rates roughly 10 to 20 percentage points below these output numbers, also mostly rising over time.[7]

While these figures are not strictly comparable, they and others used above suggest that success rates for aid effectiveness tend to range from 50 to 80 percent satisfactory. The impression given here is that aid tends to be ineffective or unsatisfactory at roughly the rate of early-stage venture capital investments. There are fewer outstanding aid successes, but the total percentages of satisfactory or better aid interventions are roughly equal to early-stage venture capital investments.

Where aid differs significantly from venture capital is in the area of sustainability. Venture capitalists assume a measure of sustainability in their successful investments, since by the time they end their support, those investments have become profitable. Aid interventions can be effective but unsustainable, especially where the political and economic environment in which the aid intervention has taken place turns adverse. And the sustainability of aid interventions has tended to be significantly lower than effectiveness. However, the one agency that estimates sustainability—the World Bank—shows a rising trend, from roughly one-half of assessed interventions during the period 1996–99 to three-fifths for the period 1999–2000.[8]

These roughest of comparisons suggest ideas for a discussion of how much effectiveness is enough. This discussion is one that the MCC will have to engage in as it attempts to demonstrate that the model on which it is based is accurate—that is, significant amounts of aid to good performers are more effective than aid promoting growth and poverty reduction, and that MCC has been an effective implementer of that model.

There is one more issue that the MCC experience raises: the tendency on the part of executive branch planners (not only in the Bush administration but in many other administrations as well) to oversell new programs to Congress and the public. The MCC was a new model for providing development aid to poor countries, based on the principles of conditionality (that is, that governments needed to have the policies to make them eligible for MCC aid) and "ownership" (that recipient governments should decide, within reasonable constraints, how their aid should be spent). The administration pitched the new program to Congress as a means of providing more effective aid over a relatively short period of time (that is, five years per compact) with relatively quick results. But these selling points failed to recognize conditions on the ground, as noted above: developing countries, especially those with limited government capacities, would need a lot of time to put into place acceptable plans for the use of MCC funds in an accountable and effective manner—considerably more time than was assumed by MCC planners.

This is not the first time a new idea in foreign aid has been oversold or has underperformed. But each time it happens, it erodes the confidence of Congress, the public, and the foreign policy community in aid in general.

President's Emergency Program for AIDS Relief: The Challenges of the Big Push

PEPFAR was established in the implicit belief that a particular problem (in this case, HIV/AIDS prevention, treatment, and care) could be addressed by allocating a very large amount of aid to deal with it—an approach reminiscent of an earlier view that had advocated a large volume of aid, a "big push," in order to spur development generally in poor countries. While different in key areas, both of these big pushes put great faith in aid as a means of resolving a complex problem, downplaying obstacles to the efficacy of aid and its potential side effects.

The argument often made by PEPFAR advocates is that the rate of infection is rising faster than the rate at which ARVs are supplied worldwide, so funding needs to be ramped up quickly to bring the problem under control. The important differences between the big push for development and that against HIV/AIDS are that (1) the latter is likely to become a permanent element in U.S. aid, given the chronic nature of HIV/AIDS and the poverty of many of its victims in the developing world; (2) a big push for development potentially engages an entire economy while PEPFAR engages only one major problem (HIV/AIDS and to a lesser extent malaria and TB) in one sector (health); and (3) a big push for one sector or function can skew U.S. development aid toward that sector and limit the ability of the administration to address major development issues more broadly.[9]

Objections to a big push approach center on the problem of diminishing returns when foreign aid increases rapidly and dramatically. Because of capacity constraints in governments or organizations receiving the aid (and even among aid agencies in developed countries providing the aid, especially if they are under pressure to spend the money), the returns on that aid could decline as bureaucrats, government management systems, and recipients are overwhelmed with funding. And there are other problems, such as aid dependence—a moral hazard when foreign assistance displaces local funding for activities that recipient governments should be covering. Sudden, large amounts of aid also discourage needed but difficult reforms and avoid hard budget constraints; they make it possible for dysfunctional leaders to remain in power and, like large returns from natural resources, make them less accountable to their publics. Behavioral disincentives also result—if the flows are large enough; government officials and others from different sectors in society may find it more remunerative to spend their time chasing aid monies than producing goods and services. Finally, the impact of aid on the economy in general can have deleterious effects where major increases in aid over a short period of time drive up inflation and exchange rates and depress exports—one variety of the famous "Dutch Disease" that has long preoccupied development economists. All of these effects of large inflows of aid are mostly theoretical since aid flows seldom reach such large volumes for individual countries, and research on diminishing returns to aid has been limited.[10]

However, many of these problems may not remain theoretical with regard to PEPFAR monies. The large and rising sums provided primarily to African governments for fighting HIV/AIDS have already begun to tax the health systems there, which have never been strong and are typically short on medical personnel, space, equipment, and drugs to address the many, many health challenges of life in the tropics. There is evidence, cited in chapter 2, of medical personnel being drawn out of general practice into the treatment of HIV/AIDS. There are already concerns being quietly expressed by U.S. Agency for International Development (USAID) personnel in the field about having too much PEPFAR funding to use it all productively. With regard to prevention, there is clearly a need to do a lot more but great uncertainty as to how to persuade Africans and others to abandon practices that have put them in danger of contracting AIDS, not to mention the women and girls who are powerless in male-dominated cultures to set the rules of their sexual encounters. The moral hazard threatened by substantial foreign funding of particular government services over an extended period of time is real as well. In short, there is an obvious capacity problem in many countries, above all in Africa, in dealing with the large and sudden increases in funding to fight HIV/AIDS.

In addition to the capacity problem, there is the broader issue of dealing with HIV/AIDS and health in a way that improves the well-being of not just AIDS victims but of societies as a whole. Health systems need to be strengthened, medical personnel paid more to keep them from immigrating to the United States and elsewhere, and hospitals need to be better built, better supplied, and better run.

And then, what happens to those victims of AIDS when they are again healthy enough to work? Should there not be programs to ensure that they can earn a living adequate not only to feed themselves and their families but also to enable them someday to pay for their own drugs? In short, there is a dense network of economic and social interrelationships in societies where, if large amounts of funding are allocated only to one problem or one sector (often called "stove-piping"), imbalances and distortions begin to appear elsewhere and eventually funding can be wasted and have a negative impact on recipient societies. The motivation and vision of PEPFAR are laudable, but the program must also address problems that are related to HIV/AIDS and that go beyond the disease itself and even beyond the health sector itself. And, it is important to note, PEPFAR is primarily a donor-driven aid program, with amounts and uses set in Washington, not a demand-driven one. There is no question recipient governments are happy to receive PEPFAR funding, but as the quantity of that funding grows, the danger arises that as PEPFAR monies increase, the problems of ownership may increase.

Finally, there is the question of balance in U.S. aid giving. The complaint is often heard that the United States does too many things with its aid and lacks focus and effectiveness. It is true that a considerable portion of U.S. bilateral aid—including Development Assistance, Child Survival and Global Health, PL 480 Food Aid, Economic Support Funds (ESF),

F I G U R E   3 - 1. U.S. Bilateral Aid and Aid for Health, 2005–08ᵃ

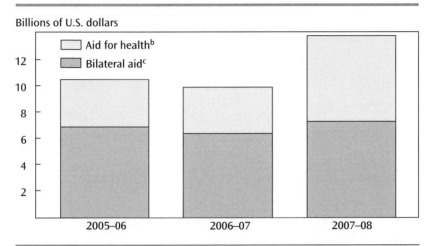

Billions of U.S. dollars

Source: Consolidated Appropriations Act, 2008 (www.cfr.org/content/publications/attachments/ 2764.pdf) and Department of State, International Affairs Budget, 2008.
a. The data are not disbursements but appropriations. Disbursements are likely to be smaller, especially for the MCC.
b. Aid for health includes the aid accounts of Child Survival and Global Health and the President's Emergency Program for AIDS Relief (PEPFAR).
c. Bilateral aid represents aid appropriated in the following major accounts: Development Assist-ance (DA), Economic Support Funds (ESF), Millennium Challenge Account (MCC), and P.L. 480 Food Aid.

and the Millennium Challenge Account—finances a variety of diverse activities, often ones that Congress has earmarked or the president has identified in a presidential initiative. But it appears increasingly to be the case that U.S. development aid is oriented toward global health issues, especially HIV/AIDS. Two major aid accounts now focus on health: the Child Survival and Global Health account ($1.8 billion in 2008) and the PEPFAR monies ($4.7 billion in 2008). These equal nearly one-half of total U.S. bilateral aid included in the five major bilateral aid accounts listed above plus PEPFAR monies—a percentage that rose significantly in 2007–08, as figure 3-1 shows—and, with current commitments to fund-ing HIV/AIDS, will continue to rise in the future.

Figure 3-2 shows the portion of aid funding from PEPFAR in 2008 in four countries as a proportion of U.S. bilateral economic assistance (Devel-opment Assistance, Child Survival and Global Health, ESF, and PEPFAR).

F I G U R E   3 - 2.   U.S. Bilateral Aid: PEPFAR and Other, 2008

Zambia

Tanzania

Haiti

☐ PEPFAR aid
■ Other bilateral aid

Kenya

Source: USAID, International Affairs Budget, Fiscal Year 2008, country aid charts (www.usaid.gov/policy/budget/cbj2008/fy2008cbj_highlights.pdf).

The number of focus countries receiving PEPFAR monies is still limited, but the charts demonstrate the potential for imbalance in those countries receiving HIV/AIDS funding.

Fighting HIV/AIDS is a worthy cause, but the amounts of funding allocated to this function threaten to limit the funding and flexibility of U.S. bilateral aid to poor countries to address development problems in a holistic fashion.

The Problem of Failed States

The greatest policy deficiency in foreign aid under the Bush administration is the absence of a policy to deal with the problems of failing and failed states. In 2002 the president's National Security Strategy of the United States declared that "America is now threatened less by conquering states than we are by failing ones."[11] Statements and reports from the Department of Defense (DoD), the Department of State, and USAID have evinced a strong concern with the consequences of fragile and failed states, which can harbor terrorists in their ungoverned spaces and whose discontented and often unemployed youth can become vulnerable to the temptations of terrorism. In addition to creating potential sources and sanctuaries for terrorists, drug dealers, and other criminal elements, state weakness or failure can block development and can lead to civil violence, producing displacement, destruction, widespread civilian deaths, and grave humanitarian crises.

As of 2008 there is still no significant or coherent U.S. policy or program to address the problems of failed states. Concern with these states has driven the Department of Defense to begin to provide economic and security assistance to stabilize weak states in Africa and elsewhere. Reflecting its own concern with these states, USAID published a policy paper entitled "Fragile States Strategy," which, however, was rather more of a statement of the problem and less a strategy for dealing with it.[12] Additionally, problems of state collapse and the task of "nation building" motivated the creation of the Coordinator for Reconstruction and Stabilization in the Department of State (S/CRS).

So what is the problem? There are several that policy planners working on failed states must tackle. How is a "failed state" to be defined? How and why does a state fail? How can state failure be prevented or reversed?

What is a Failing and Failed State?

Establishing an accepted meaning of "failing and failed states" is the first step in identifying a policy response. There are several definitional problems. The first is that different scholars, think tanks, and government agencies use the term in quite distinct ways depending on the problems within these states that concern them. At present, different terms are used to describe these states, including weak states, low-income states, poorly performing states, difficult partners, and fragile states. And these terms are often used interchangeably. The London-based Overseas Development Institute in a recent report on fragile states observed that "The term 'fragile states' has no precise meaning" and went on to point out that the term has been used to describe the *functionality* of states—are they able to provide security, basic services (education, health), effective economic regulation?—as well as the *consequences* of state fragility—that is, the problems they create, such as global security threats or refugees.[13] Box 3-1 lays out the major components of fragile states, assumptions on causality, approaches to addressing them, and which government agencies employ them.

There have also been several approaches to measuring the degree of state fragility or failure. One attempt has involved identifying and measuring gaps between the expected functions of states and what they really do. The greater the gap between the expected and actual functions, the greater the fragility of the state.[14] Another approach, reflected in the Index of Failed States produced by the Fund for Peace and *Foreign Policy* magazine, identified a set of factors believed to contribute to state fragility, rated countries on those factors, and produced a list of failed states (see box 3-2).

Clearly, even these two approaches reflect very different ideas of state failure. The gap analysis permits a distinction between failed and failing states, with failed states presumably unable to perform most or all the normal functions of a state. Somalia would be a completely failed—or collapsed—state. In the index approach, there is no special category for a collapsed state; rather, states with serious problems are all classified as more or less failed.

What are we to make of the confusion in the use of the terms weak, fragile, failing, and failed states? The best thing is to ignore the terms and simply identify what our main concern is with the performance of states and develop our policies and programs accordingly. The Bush administration's main concern with regard to failing and failed states is their potential role in harboring terrorists. Many in the U.S. government and policy community have also long been concerned about the developmental and humanitarian consequences of state failure, but what has elevated state failure to a priority today is the global war on terror. The next administration will need to elaborate a policy reflecting that priority, and this section offers some thoughts on how to proceed.

Tackling Fragile and Failed States

There are four types of problems related to the behavior of governments that can produce sanctuaries for terrorists. I shall use four different terms

BOX 3-1. Main Components of the Fragile States Agenda

Focus or emphasis and goals	Underlying assumptions and views on causality	Types of "external" actors and approaches	Donors emphasizing a particular component of the FS agenda
Local peace, human security, and basic needs	Politicization of ethnic and religious divisions and of resource constraints causes conflict, which undermines development.	Postconflict resolution specialists, peace-keeping agencies focusing on IDPs and refugees, security-sector reform, DDR and development, and humanitarian workers	DFID UN peace-keeping BMZ EU
Economic development and good governance	State failure, collapse, weakness, underperformance causes poor developmental outcomes and vice-versa. Differences in emphasis on ◆ Economic and political development ◆ Governance as primary driver or consequence of economic growth ◆ Short-term humanitarian needs or longer-term development aims	Range of developmental and humanitarian professionals and donor agencies, including bilateral agencies, UN, IFIs, economic analysts, and governance and human rights workers	DFID Aus-AID USAID UNDP IFIs OECD-DAC BMZ Netherlands agencies EC
Global security	The poor quality of governance and the economy in some weak states generates organized crime (for example, drug trade), terrorism, immigration and social cohesion concerns, WMD threats, and so on. Development and good governance in these countries are instrumental to reducing global security threats.	Foreign policy and diplomacy, security and defense actors, police, anti–drug trafficking, money laundering, arms specialists.	United States (DoD, State Department and USAID) United Kingdom (FCP and MoD) Aus-AID UN Security Council OECD EC

Source: Diana Cammack, Dinah McLeod, and Alina Rocha Menocal with Karin Christiansen, *Donors and the "Fragile States" Agenda: A Survey of Current Thinking and Practice* (London: Overseas Development Institute, 2006), p. x.

B O X   3 - 2 .   Failed States and Their Indicators

Social indicators

Mounting demographic pressures
Massive movement of refugees or internally displaced persons creating
    complex humanitarian emergencies
Legacy of vengeance-seeking group grievance or group paranoia
Chronic and sustained human flight

Economic indicator

Uneven economic development along group lines
Sharp or severe economic decline, or both

Political indicators

Criminalization or delegitimization of the state, or both
Progressive deterioration of public services
Suspension or arbitrary application of the rule of law and widespread
    violation of human rights
Security apparatus operates as a "state within a state"
Rise of factionalized elites
Intervention of other states or external political actors

Worst cases of failed states[a]

Sudan	Pakistan	Sierra Leone
Iraq	North Korea	Yemen
Somalia	Myanmar	Sri Lanka
Zimbabwe	Uganda	Republic of the Congo
Chad	Bangladesh	Liberia
Côte d'Ivoire	Nigeria	Lebanon
Democratic Republic of the Congo	Ethiopia	Malawi
Afghanistan	Burundi	Solomon Islands
Guinea	Timor-Leste	Kenya
Central African Republic	Nepal	Niger
Haiti	Uzbekistan	

Source: This box is drawn from the Fund for Peace (www.fundforpeace.org/web/index.php?
option=com_content&task=view&id=229&Itemid=366).
    a. This list represents the top 32 worst cases of failed states on the basis of their scores on
the Failed States Index 2007 (from first to thirty-second).

drawn from the state failure discourse to describe them. First are *weak or fragile states* that do not have a large enough or competent enough military or security services to govern their space, such as many in the Sahelian region of Africa. These states are typically very poor with responsibilities for securing very large (and often sparsely populated) spaces. Theirs is a *capacity* problem.

Second, there are *failing states* that are so oppressive or corrupt that—while their security services may not be weak and they may not have ungoverned spaces—their behavior drives their societies toward conflict and eventual state collapse (for example, Zimbabwe, Myanmar, or Liberia under Charles Taylor), which can produce ungoverned spaces. Their problem is a *governance* problem.

Third are *rogue states* that might be able to control their territory and deliver some services to their populations but choose to harbor or tolerate terrorists operating within their borders, such as Afghanistan under the Taliban, Sudan, and perhaps Pakistan. Finally, there are *collapsed states* that are largely or wholly nonfunctional. These types of states are typically the result of prolonged periods of poor governance, often combined with external interference; they almost always experience widespread violence and civil conflict and have ungoverned spaces or spaces where warlords or militias operate. Somalia has long been the poster child for a collapsed state. The Democratic Republic of the Congo, Guinea, and Sudan may be headed in the same direction.

What Makes States Weak, Failing, and Failed?

All states have weaknesses. But which weaknesses lead to failure and why? With all the differences in definitions of failed and failing states, it is no surprise that there has been a lot of research and debate on why states are weak or failing, but there are no settled answers. One approach is to list the conditions that are presumed to contribute to state weakness and then attempt to measure them, as with the Index of Failed States.

Another approach has been to identify the main factors that are correlated with state failure. This was the methodology behind the State Failure Project, first commissioned by the Clinton administration in 1994 and later continued at the University of Maryland and George Mason

University.[15] The first findings of this study, based on an extensive analysis of available data associated with severe political crises, found that three factors were correlated with state failure: closed trading systems, high childhood mortality rates, and the absence of democracy. Trade is associated with economic performance; childhood mortality rates are a result of the services states provide; and democracy is linked to the ability of citizens to have their voices heard and have government protect and promote their interests. These efforts at identifying and accumulating quantitative indicators and correlating them with state failure are useful in providing a general impression of the underlying weaknesses of states, but they do not tell us why some weak states sometimes progress to failing and failed states. Nor do they give us the tools to predict when failure and collapse looms.

One way to understand the dynamics of state failure is suggested by the State Failure Project. Clearly underlying conditions increase the likelihood of state failure generally, such as poverty, lack of education and infrastructure, and perhaps ethnic or religious cleavages. But many states with these conditions do not descend into failure. Additionally, accelerators of state failure, for example, political repression, pervasive corruption, economic exclusion, and past experience of civil conflict, can create a predisposition of societal groups toward conflict. But states can exist in a position of fragility and even increasing weakness without dissolving into failure or violence. Finally, there are triggers of state failure. External intervention is often a factor and one far too little considered in studies of failing and failed states. Other factors are a severe economic shock, natural disaster, or a major political crisis, or very poor decisions on the part of political leaders.

While this three-part structure does not provide a satisfactory theory of state failure, it does begin to provide a framework for studying past cases of state weakness and collapse and suggests a direction for U.S. policies to address these problems. The underlying conditions help explain why weak states lack the capacity to control their spaces, even though they want to do so and may be governed relatively well. Their poverty and high unemployment may lead young people with few life prospects to become terrorist recruits. Clearly, poverty and unemployment are not the only factors leading to terrorist recruitment; sometimes, as with the 9/11 terrorists, they play no obvious role at all. A deep sense of humiliation or injustice can also have an impact.

What Is to Be Done?

The underlying conditions of weak states can be addressed with traditional long-term development programs managed by USAID and could also include aid and training to strengthen local security forces where they are weak.

Weak states can turn into failing states where political elites are corrupt or repressive. Corruption and repression can act as accelerators by undercutting the legitimacy of the state—especially where one ethnic or religious group is favored and others are excluded. Exclusion and repression also can make states vulnerable to civil conflict and failure. These states may or may not have ungoverned spaces, but the real problem is the way they are governed. Thus, strengthening their militaries could make the problems of repression and, perhaps, corruption worse. To change their manner of governing requires persuasion, pressure (including carrots and sticks), and even military intervention—all preferably on a multilateral basis. Aid can be used as an incentive, in coordination with other aid-giving governments and institutions, but it is seldom adequate alone; and unless used judiciously, aid can even be counterproductive. In some cases, foreign governments may have no leverage over the political leadership, as in the case of Zimbabwe or Myanmar. Military intervention (direct or indirect), as we have seen in Iraq, can bring its own set of intractable problems. In the end, there may be no good policy options while that leadership is in power.

Triggering factors are by their nature unpredictable, but one factor in particular is vulnerable to policy action—the role of external actors, including states as well as non-state actors that play a role provoking and funding civil violence in weak states. For example, Muammar Qaddafi of Libya is said to have been deeply involved in multiple cases of civil violence and state failure in West Africa. In the Horn of Africa, the axis of conflict has been between Sudan, Eritrea, Ethiopia, and Uganda where various governments have armed and supported rebels in neighboring countries to weaken their governments and strengthen the bargaining position of the intervening state on issues of conflict. A regional perspective and response is essential in addressing the problems of failing states.

Dealing with rogue states is a diplomatic and military task where foreign aid might play a limited role as an incentive for behavioral change. Helping collapsed states in the wake of civil conflict or war involves a series of postconflict policies like disarmament, demobilization, and reintegration as well as nation building, especially where there is a U.S. military occupation. There are two units in the U.S. government available for this work: the Office of Transition Initiatives in USAID and the S/CRS office in the Department of State. There may also be a role for DoD if the U.S. military is an occupying power or is otherwise involved. These functions need to be elaborated and integrated with more attention on what works and what does not and at what cost to the United States.

The thrust of this discussion on failed states is not so much to suggest a set of U.S. policies but to argue that we need to be clear about the problems weak states present us with and to begin developing our policies from that point rather than act as if there is a coherent category of "fragile, failing, or failed states" that we can and must change and reform.

One More Element in Aid's Transformation

Much of the discussion thus far has been about the problems associated with the transformation in foreign aid undertaken over the past seven years. It is worth ending this chapter with a brief mention of an initiative that holds considerable promise—the Office of Global Development Alliances (GDA), housed in USAID, which supports private-public partnerships, including business enterprises, foundations, and nonprofit agencies, to promote international development. The partnerships typically involve joint design, planning, and implementation through a collaboration agreement (different from a contract or grant from USAID where the agency is in the driver's seat). By September 2007 USAID had formed 600 alliances, leveraging $5.8 billion in resources from partners with a U.S. government investment of $2.1 billion.[16] Past alliances among USAID, the World Cocoa Federation, and the chocolate industry have helped African

BOX 3-3. Roles of the members of the Sustainable Forest Products Global Alliance

◆ U.S. Agency for International Development (USAID) provides funds and manages the alliance.
◆ The World Wildlife Fund manages the Global Forest and Trade Network, an affiliation of national and regional buyer and producer groups in nearly thirty nations, with more than 400 member companies committed to responsible forestry.
◆ Metafore works with North American businesses to promote the responsible purchasing and use of wood and paper.
◆ The U.S. Department of Agriculture (USDA) Forest Service provides technical support and guidance.
◆ Home Depot, a charter private sector partner, contributes funding, its global reputation, and its purchasing model in support of responsible forest management.

Source: USAID, Office of Global Development Alliances, "Global Development Alliance: Public-Private Alliances for Transformational Development," Washington, January 2006 (www.usaid.gov/our_work/global_partnerships/gda/pdf/GDA_Report_Jan2006_Intro.pdf).

cocoa farmers to upgrade the quality of their product while protecting biodiversity. The Sustainable Forest Products Alliance encourages responsible logging practices and forest management through a certification program and technical assistance. Box 3-3 describes the roles of the various members of this particular alliance.

The GDA represents an innovation that is an increasing trend in the twenty-first century: reaching out to the many private enterprises and foundations that already play an important role in development—a role that only promises to expand. The model is now being imitated by the MCC, the International Finance Corporation, and other public aid agencies.

Summing Up

The aid initiatives of the Bush administration are both worthy and laudable. But they raise basic issues, many of which are familiar in other forms to development practitioners. The MCC is essentially an experiment with a new business model for using aid effectively to further development. It is not yet clear that this model will work as expected, at least within the political time frame that exists in Washington.

The experience of PEPFAR raises a different warning flag—that very large amounts of funding for a particular functional program can distort overall development progress in recipient countries. There is the additional concern that the overall U.S. aid program can become unbalanced.

Finally, the discussion of fragile states suggests another familiar lesson of past experience in aid giving. Where new policy concerns in aid giving arise with little settled meaning behind them or limited ideas of how to address them (as with sustainable development or conflict prevention in the 1990s), they become fads but ultimately have little impact on the use or effectiveness of aid. Without considerably more clarity in our thinking about fragile and failed states, aid to address "state fragility" may prove to be one of these fads, except, in this case, a powerful department— DoD—is poised to deploy an increasing amount of aid to tackle this as yet poorly defined purpose.

FOUR

Issues of Organization and Change Management

The process of transforming President Bush's foreign aid has highlighted the challenges of undertaking major policy and organizational reforms in the public sector—challenges that are relevant to the further initiatives in U.S. foreign aid that must come in the future.

Issues of Organization

The creation or emergence of three new sources of bilateral aid—the Millennium Challenge Corporation (MCC), the President's Emergency Plan for AIDS Response (PEPFAR), and the Department of Defense (DoD)—have added to the fragmentation of the aid system within the U.S. government. Whereas there was one main bilateral development aid agency in the past, there are now two major aid agencies managing bilateral aid—MCC and the U.S. Agency for International Development (USAID), which has integrated its planning and budgeting with the Department of State. And with DoD's growing economic assistance, perhaps a third is in the making. In addition, one very large bilateral aid program—PEPFAR—is headquartered in the State Department. More than twenty small aid programs are located in other U.S. government agencies. And the Department of the Treasury has responsibilities for U.S. contributions to the international financial institutions. Each of these programs and agencies has valuable and distinct missions, but many overlap with one another, creating the real possibility—indeed, the inevitability—of duplication, conflict, waste, confused leadership, and lost synergies. And the integration of planning and budgeting of USAID and the Department of State raises the possibility that at some point the mission of State—larger, more powerful, and more driven by short-term crises—will overwhelm the longer-term mission of the smaller, less powerful USAID.

The current organizational chaos is surely costly and unsustainable. What alternatives are there to reordering these agencies and programs to reduce the organizational chaos and exploit potential synergies? This question has four parts: (1) Which aid programs and agencies could be combined or separated? (2) What alternatives are there for locating them in the bureaucratic pecking order: as part of an existing federal department? As a subcabinet-level development agency? As a new cabinet-level department? (3) How can coordination problems among agencies and programs that work on similar issues or operate in the same countries be managed? (4) And what are the political costs associated with alternative organizational models? This latter issue cannot be ignored in any discussion of organizational change in the public sector.

How Should Foreign Aid Be Organized?

The first item to consider in bringing greater order to the current chaotic system is which aid programs should be located together, and, behind that question, what criteria should be used to decide on co-location or separation? In the past, various government commissions have typically recommended grouping government programs with similar purposes or functions into common departments and agencies for maximum efficiencies and effectiveness. For example, in 1949 the Commission on the Organization of the Executive Branch of Government (also known as the Hoover Commission, from Herbert Hoover, its chair) observed, "There are too many separate agencies, several of which are not combined in accordance with their major purpose. . . . The numerous agencies of the executive branch must be grouped into departments as nearly as possible by major purposes in order to give a coherent mission to each department."[1] Many scholars of public administration have echoed these views.[2] The notion, drawn from architecture, that form should follow function (or purpose in the case of public policies) has been challenged, but as yet no other basic criterion for organizing government has emerged.[3]

But the notion of function or purpose is used in different ways in current debates involving the organization of foreign aid and U.S. affairs agencies generally. For some, mainly in the foreign policy community, purpose is seen as the promotion of U.S. foreign policy generally. They further argue that policies and programs (including foreign aid) should be aligned and organized appropriately to further this purpose. In organizational terms, they tend to favor integrating foreign aid programs to the maximum extent possible within the Department of State.

Others—this author among them—argue that this concept of purpose is too broad to be the basis of organizational decisions; that "U.S. foreign policy" includes a variety of discrete objectives that are ends in themselves, some of which can conflict with others, and that these distinct objectives or purposes require separate organizations for their effective realization. For example, a core purpose within the broad category of furthering U.S. foreign policy is managing bilateral relations with other governments. Another important purpose is promoting development in poor countries. The first tends to involve primarily government-to-government relations, to have a short-term focus, and often to involve dealing with crises in relations with other governments. The second typically involves an array of civil society and other nongovernmental organizations as well as government ministries and has necessarily a long-term horizon needed to bring about beneficial change in another society.

These two imperatives can conflict when the imperatives of managing a short-term crisis require aid resources to bolster a U.S. negotiating posture—for example, as a *quid pro quo*; to signal approval or disapproval of another government's actions; to provide access to key policymakers in another government; or just to ensure friendly relations. These imperatives can draw aid resources out of development work and at times undercut that work—for instance, when aid to corrupt or incompetent governments reduces their incentives to undertake painful but needed economic or political reforms. It has long been believed by development practitioners as well as by experienced U.S. diplomats, for example, that the large amount of U.S. aid to Egypt over an extended period of time has reduced the incentives for that government to reform its state-directed economy.[4] Where there are potentially significant conflicts between two programs with distinct but different aims—even though at the broadest level they serve the same long-term objectives—there is an argument for ensuring they are separately administered; at the same time, mechanisms should be put in place to ensure effective coordination between the two.

Another criterion for organizational decisions involves the nature of the tasks performed by professionals. Where the knowledge, skills, and experience required to undertake core organizational tasks differ substantially, separate personnel systems and a separate organization may be necessary. Again, in the case of foreign aid, the tasks of program management—planning, procuring needed services, providing oversight, and evaluating aid expenditures—are fundamentally different from the tasks of a foreign affairs ministry, which typically involve reporting, analysis, negotiation, and representation. (The recent debacle over the State Department oversight of contracts with Blackwater Security Services in Iraq is a mistake easily made by an agency not experienced in large-scale program management.) Professionals in these two areas of diplomacy and development cannot easily be substituted for one another—a fact recognized by most aid-giving governments that typically maintain distinct personnel systems for diplomatic and development professionals (see box 4-1).

It is important to revisit here a related organizational consideration touched on in chapter 2—the relationship between policies determining the *allocation of the aid* to individual countries (by which is meant rules or guidelines determining which countries receive aid and how much they receive) and guidelines and rules governing the *use and implementation of aid funding*—for example, for education, health, economic reform, agriculture, as well as procurement, field supervision, and evaluation of these uses. Where the primary purpose of the allocation of aid to countries is diplomatic, but the implementation of that aid is linked to development goals, it is possible to separate policy from implementation and place them in separate agencies as some of the governments in box 4-1 have done. This has, in effect, been the arrangement in the United States with Economic Support Funds (ESF) and the Andean Counter-drug Initiative over the past several decades: State takes the lead in deciding which countries get the aid funding and how much they get, usually based on foreign policy goals such as peace making in the Middle East or persuading Andean governments to suppress the production of coca, and USAID takes the lead in determining how the aid is spent and implements those decisions. Dividing policy from implementation is not an ideal organizational arrangement—the learning that comes from the practical experience of implementation often can be

B O X   4 - 1 . Aid Policy and Implementation in Other Governments

The government of Japan locates aid allocation policy in the Ministry of Foreign Affairs with implementation undertaken by two separate aid agencies (Japan Bank for International Cooperation and Japan International Cooperation Agency, now in the process of merging into one implementing agency).

The **German** government locates development policy in the Ministry of Development with implementation also undertaken by two aid agencies.

The government of the **United Kingdom** combines all of its aid programs as well as policy and implementation responsibilities in one place—the Department for International Development.

The **French** government has a subcabinet-level aid agency (Agence Française de Développement) that takes policy guidance from the Ministries of Finance and Foreign Affairs and manages much of French aid.

Some governments, like those of **Denmark** and the **Netherlands,** fully merge their aid and foreign affairs functions. It is worth noting that promoting development is often the major diplomatic interest of these governments in most poor countries

For more details on the aid programs and organization of individual donor governments, see the series of peer reviews of aid activities of members of the Development Assistance Committee of the Organization for Economic Cooperation and Development (www.oecd.org).

absent from policy decisions, risking the overall effectiveness of the effort. But where there are several major purposes driving individual country aid programs, there may be no better alternative.[5]

If it is accepted that in the U.S. government it makes sense to have a separate agency dedicated to using aid for development, which programs should be located there? Box 4-2 lists the major programs in U.S. aid-giving at present. If we combine those aid accounts that have as their primary goals the overlapping purposes of providing relief, encouraging development, and addressing global issues, those with asterisks would be co-located into a rationalized development agency. Aid for international organizations and programs, now located primarily in the Department of State, represents voluntary U.S. contributions, mainly to United Nations organizations. Where those organizations' main work is in relief or development, like the UN Development Program or the UN Children's

---

B O X   4 - 2 . Major U.S. Aid Accounts: Policy and Implementation Responsibilities

Development Assistance (USAID)*
Child Survival and Global Health (USAID)*
P.L. 480 Food Aid (Titles II and III) (Agriculture/USAID)*
Assistance for Eastern Europe and the Baltic States (State/USAID)*
Assistance for the Independent States of the Former Soviet Union (State/USAID)*
Migration and Refugee Assistance (State/USAID)*
Global HIV/AIDS Initiative (State-PEPFAR/USAID, other agencies)*
International Organizations and Programs (State/USAID, other agencies/ implementation by international organizations)*
Millennium Challenge Account (Millennium Challenge Corporation)*
Multilateral Aid (Treasury Department; implementation by international financial institutions)*
Department of Defense Aid (DoD)
Economic Support Fund (State/USAID)
Andean Counter-drug Initiative (State/USAID)

---

*Policymaking/implementing agency (or agencies) in parentheses.

Emergency Fund (UNICEF), responsibility for these contributions should be located in the aid agency. Multilateral aid programs include the World Bank, the Asian Development Bank, the Inter-American Development Bank, the African Development Bank and Fund, and a number of smaller international development programs. These are all part of a U.S. effort to give aid for development through international financial institutions; it makes sense to co-locate responsibilities for them with other aid programs, as a number of other governments do. Policy responsibility for assistance for continuing transitions in former Soviet bloc countries (including country allocation and use of aid) should also be shifted to a development agency since most of those countries still receiving aid are among the poorer ones in Eastern Europe and in the former Soviet Union and much of what the aid finances corresponds to what is done in poorer countries in other parts of the world.

Finally, it is important that a development agency should not just manage aid but also have a voice in U.S. government policies and programs related to those purposes. Trade, finance (including debt relief), and investment are good examples. A development agency should have expertise and a degree of involvement (though not the lead) in these other aspects of international development if it is to be effective abroad and influential at home. This, again, is a practice evident in other governments, as in the United Kingdom and Germany.

Policy responsibilities for ESF (with its purpose clarified as primarily supporting U.S. diplomatic and security goals abroad) and the Andean Counter-drug Initiative would remain in the Department of State. The case of DoD economic assistance may be similar to the relationship of ESF in the Department of State to a development agency. If DoD moves forward in providing aid to help stabilize poor countries in Africa and elsewhere or to finance good works outside of combat zones, the implementation of these efforts can be undertaken by the development agency that has the professional expertise and the programming systems to do so. It may make sense for DoD to allocate aid monies to help stabilize fragile states (once we have a settled policy on who they are and how to help them), but it is questionable whether Defense should set up its own aid program with all the planning, implementation, evaluation, and coordination with other U.S. government agencies that such a program implies.

This effort to imagine a rationalized organization of major U.S. programs promoting development has left out the many smaller aid programs—often involving the funding of technical advice to foreign governments—operated by most U.S. government departments. The departments and agencies with smaller aid programs as of 2005 are listed in box 4-3. In an ideal organizational world, those programs of the agencies listed here that could reasonably be considered as having a primary purpose of relief and development and global issues would also be included in a rationalized development agency.

Location within the Bureaucracy

The location of a program or agency determines its authority, its role, its influence, and its status. Clearly, cabinet-level agencies, which report directly to the president, have the greatest authority and influence. They do not take orders from other cabinet-level agencies, and irresolvable disputes

BOX 4-3. U.S. Government Agencies with Foreign Aid Programs

African Development Foundation

Department of Agriculture
Agricultural Research Service (ARS)
Animal and Plant Health Inspection Service (APHIS)
Cooperative State Research Education and Extension Service (CSREES)
Foreign Agricultural Service (FAS)
Forest Service (FS)

Department of Commerce
U.S. Patent and Trademark Office (PTO)
Commercial Law Development Program (CLDP)
International Trade Administration (ITA)
National Institute of Standards and Technology (NIST)
National Oceanic and Atmospheric Administration (NOAA)

Department of Energy

Department of Health and Human Services
Centers for Disease Control and Prevention

Department of Homeland Security
U.S. Customs and Border Protection

Department of the Interior
Compact of Free Association
U.S. Fish and Wildlife Service

Department of Justice

Department of Labor

Department of Transportation

Environmental Protection Agency

Export-Import Bank

Federal Trade Commission

Inter-American Foundation

National Endowment for Democracy

Overseas Private Investment Corporation

Peace Corps

U.S. Trade and Development Agency

Source: USAID, *Overseas Loans and Grants* (http://qesdb.usaid.gov/gbk/USG%20Organizatons. html [August 2007]).

between such agencies are typically mediated by the president. Federal departments typically have lead policy, programmatic, and budgetary authorities over their core areas of responsibility; they can convene other parts of the government on their issues; they are accountable to Congress for their areas of policy responsibility, and they represent the U.S. government on those policy issues at home and abroad. They can usually fend off efforts by other agencies to influence or control their budgets and policies.

Where subcabinet-level agencies are accountable to cabinet-level agencies, they may not have a clear lead in their core areas of responsibility, and they may lack effective convening power and authority to coordinate other agencies' policies in those areas. Indeed, at times, they may not even be invited to the table where discussions among cabinet agency representatives are taking place on relevant issues. (Excluding agencies from important interagency meetings is an old game in Washington; it is a lot easier to do when subcabinet agencies are involved.) Subcabinet-level organizations will typically have control over their budget and personnel systems, though where they report to a cabinet-level agency, they may have to negotiate their budget with that agency. They will have some political space to maneuver among more powerful government agencies that might wish to influence or control their policies and budgets.

There are three options for organizing U.S. foreign aid and, in particular, development aid. The major programs focusing primarily on humanitarian relief and the promotion of economic, political, and social development abroad could be united into a single agency located (1) at the cabinet level; (2) at the subcabinet level; or (3) fully merged into the Department of State. What are the criteria that should govern this critical organizational decision in the United States?

The principal justification for creating a cabinet-level development agency is that the purpose and mission of promoting development abroad is of sufficient importance, size, and scope that it should be raised to this level. That the Bush administration has emphasized a troika of defense, diplomacy, and development as major elements in the U.S. approach to foreign affairs implies that development is worthy of a cabinet-level position. This is strongly supported by many in the U.S. development community. Of course, others might argue that promoting development abroad does not enjoy a sufficient stature, scope of activity, or priority to justify its location in a new federal department. Further, there is a widely shared view in the foreign policy community that development aid should remain in a supporting role, closely linked to U.S. diplomacy. In this view, creating a cabinet-level department for development aid would give such an agency too much independence from the Department of State.

The issue of whether the scope of development is significant enough and of a high enough priority to warrant its location in a cabinet-level agency is a judgment call. There are no set criteria or benchmarks for deciding this issue. While in the past international development has not been given a high priority in U.S. foreign policy and has not enjoyed the sizeable budgets and numbers of employees a cabinet-level agency would seem to imply, recent large increases in U.S. aid might change that perspective. The 2007 requested budget for the development programs listed in box 4-2—USAID, MCC, PEPFAR, and other aid programs in the Department of State—amounted to just over $11 billion. This was all discretionary spending—that is, not mandated by law. As mentioned earlier in this study, discretionary expenditures represent roughly one-third of total U.S. government budgetary expenditures per year. If we compare that level of spending to the levels of discretionary spending on the part of existing cabinet agencies, we find that the departments of Commerce, Interior, Labor, and Treasury are at the same or lower levels of such spending. It should be noted that when mandatory spending is added to these budgets, they tend to double in size. (There is no mandatory spending associated with foreign aid.) These data suggest that at least in terms of annual discretionary spending budgets, a cabinet-level development agency would be among the smaller of such agencies but not so small as to be an anomaly.

Those supporting a cabinet-level development agency might also argue that even if the scope and priority of international development work abroad are relatively small, simply creating such an agency would provide an opportunity and incentive for U.S. engagement in development to increase. Agencies are good at lobbying for their missions and budgets, and cabinet agencies are among the most influential and effective.[6] They are also often populated by competent and politically influential leaders, which is not always the case with subcabinet-level agencies where leadership positions are not as visible and are often offered as political patronage to individuals with less knowledge, experience, and leadership skills than those appointed to cabinet-level positions.

A semi-independent, subcabinet-level development agency, much as USAID has been over the past forty-five years, has its own advantages. It enjoys a degree of autonomy in pursuing its mission, but its relationship to the State Department can ensure a measure of policy consistency and coherence between the two agencies in the field. That relationship can be based on joint planning exercises for country goals; it can involve the ambassadors in the field and the secretary of state having to sign off on annual country aid budgets, as was usually the case in the past; it also can involve personnel exchanges, although this has rarely occurred between USAID and State, in large part because the training and experience of the two personnel services are quite different. However, for an aid agency to retain a measure of autonomy, it must retain authority over its budget, planning, and personnel systems, and must have some avenue of appeal—ultimately to the president if necessary—over decisions affecting it made by other agencies. A partial merger of agencies, as is the case with USAID and State, especially regarding the budget function, begins to compromise that autonomy.

Arguments for a full merger of all development programs into the Department of State are typically based on creating greater coherence between what is done to promote development and what is done to promote foreign policy generally. In a government where those two purposes are largely coincident, a merger may make sense. But where they diverge, as in cases where aid-giving governments pursue international security and political goals in developing countries distinct from development goals—as with most major powers—a full merger can lead to the purpose of the more powerful agency eventually overwhelming that of the smaller one or leading to its neglect. For example, the merger of the former U.S. Information Agency into the Department of State has, in the view of many, led to a significant downgrading of public diplomacy and cultural affairs in U.S. foreign policy. Similarly, the merger of the Federal Emergency Management Agency into the Department of Homeland Security has been blamed for weakening U.S. disaster preparedness.[7]

Interagency Coordination

For government policies and programs involving broadly similar issues but operating out of different bureaus, agencies, or departments, systems of coordination are required to ensure consistency. For instance, the need for a "whole of government" approach to address the global war on terror or failing and failed states has become more prominent as these issues have grown in importance, but they are only some of the numerous international problems requiring effective interagency coordination in an integrating and rapidly changing world.[8] The main point of policy and programmatic coordination in all development work is the U.S. ambassador in the field who leads the country team, helps develop the U.S. government mission statement for his country, and reviews overall plans for U.S. engagement there. He or she also controls who from the U.S. government can visit the country. But to leave U.S. ambassadors in the field as the principal point of interagency coordination and control in the country is risky because of the large and increasing engagement of U.S. government agencies abroad and the growing numbers of activities with a regional or sector focus (where individual countries are not the key focus of action). U.S. ambassadors have a difficult time even knowing all the U.S. government activities taking place in their countries today; those activities are only likely to expand in the future. There should be effective points of coordination in Washington as well.

In the past, interagency groups or teams have met periodically to discuss ongoing issues or have been called together to address particular challenges or crises. Problems with these arrangements have included a failure to share relevant information; decisions not made or enforced; and the slowness and time-consuming nature of the process. Behind these problems is the inevitable tendency on the part of representatives from different agencies to act primarily to protect and advance the interests of their own institutions. If interagency coordination in the future is to be more effective, new models are needed with compelling incentives for cooperation across agencies.

There are several coordinating arrangements in the defense and security areas that are worth considering for future interagency involvement in development work. One is the National Counterterrorism Center

(NCTC).[9] This organization, which reports to the director of national intelligence, serves "as the primary organization for strategic operational planning for counter-terrorism. Operating under the policy direction of the President of the United States, the National Security Council, and the Homeland Security Council, NCTC provides a full-time interagency forum and process to plan, integrate, assign lead operational roles and responsibilities, and measure the effectiveness of strategic operational counter-terrorism activities of the U.S. Government, applying all instruments of national power to the counter-terrorism mission."[10] In effect, it is an agency set up to coordinate other agencies. The NCTC draws its staff from all the agencies involved in counterterrorism activities. One could imagine a similar agency created for development within the U.S. government—to gather information on all U.S. aid and other relevant policies, help develop strategic plans for countries and regions, and assess the effectiveness of the totality of U.S. government activities in support of development. It could report to the National Security Council and the secretary of state (which would enhance its power and legitimacy) and draw a portion of its staff to serve for fixed periods from agencies engaged in aid-related activities.

Another model for interagency coordination, also drawn from the Defense Department, is the Quadrennial Defense Review (QDR). DoD undertakes this review every four years to "conduct a comprehensive examination . . . of the national defense strategy, force structure, force modernization plans, infrastructure, budget plan, and other elements of the defense program and policies of the United States with a view toward determining and expressing the defense strategy of the United States and establishing a defense program for the next 20 years."[11] One could imagine substituting development for defense, substituting the various tools of development for the tools of defense, and engaging all major agencies involved with development work under the leadership of the National Security Council. The exercise would produce an overall strategy for collaboration and coordination on countries, regions, and sectors by agencies involved in development-oriented activities.

The F process represents yet another model for interagency coordination. Ultimately, the director of U.S. foreign assistance would not only control most of the aid budgets of USAID and State but also those of all other U.S. aid programs, in effect shifting key decisionmaking authorities to the Department of State. One could also imagine overall control, coordination, and budgetary authorities lodged with the National Security Council or other elements of the White House, although this scenario would bring program responsibilities into the White House—something past administrations have tried to avoid given the brokering roles White House staff often play.

These models of interagency coordination may not be the answers to the challenge of managing aid to promote development in the future, but they can provide a starting point for thinking about the problem, which will only get worse as more U.S. government agencies become involved in attempting to improve the human condition in developing countries.

The Politics of Organization

One of the most insightful scholars of the politics of bureaucratic structure, Terry Moe, states, "Structural choices have important consequences for the content and direction of policy, and political actors know it. When they make choices about structure, they are implicitly making choices about policy."[12] This is because structure affects who decides policy and who has the authority to veto policy proposals. It involves the key decisions on budgets and personnel appointments, which ultimately affect who controls an agency and its policy decisions. It determines who has access to the decisionmakers and thus the opportunity to influence them, as well as who implements, monitors and evaluates them. The highly political nature of organizational decisions is often ignored in discussions in policy or academic circles on aid organization—it is too often assumed that the way government is organized is basically a technical issue. It is only partly that.

The politics of organization can affect foreign aid in two ways. One is the politics of where the responsibility for managing aid is placed. As noted above, if aid for development is placed in an agency whose main mission is not development, it is very likely that the aid will eventually come to support the primary mission of the home agency, whatever the original intent of those who designed the organizational arrangements.

The other dimension of the politics of organization involves organizational change. Listed earlier in this chapter are the many U.S. government agencies now running aid programs. In an ideal world, as noted, those most closely associated with development, broadly defined, should logically be placed in a development aid agency. But there are political costs to any significant organizational change. Most of the small programs scattered throughout the U.S. government are now well established in a variety of U.S. government departments with their own staffs and budgets, often supported by outside interest groups and staff and members of Congress, and are likely to be jealously protected by their agency leadership and constituents. Past proposals for shifting responsibilities for the international financial institutions from Treasury to USAID have always been effectively resisted by successive Treasury secretaries.

Major structural changes in government—for example, the merger or reconfiguration of agencies— will require legislation. And the more extensive the legislative changes, the more politically costly it becomes to the administration to get such legislation through Congress. Foreign aid is not a popular program with much of the American public and has a relatively weak constituency. Thus, members of Congress have been reluctant to vote for it unless it is absolutely necessary (for example, for appropriations legislation) or brings benefits to their constituents (usually in the form of legislative earmarks or directives). To get any new aid authorizing legislation through Congress requires presidential involvement: persuasion, arm twisting, and policy concessions that take time and often resources. Time and political capital are surely the scarcest of resources for presidents, so major reorganizations need to carry a compelling priority and the promise of major benefits to engage a president's attention and involvement.

Applying these lessons to the three major alternatives for reorganizing U.S. development aid, the most politically costly would be establishing a cabinet-level department of development. The least costly would be to leave things alone or to make organizational changes that do not require legislation or are so minor that they do not provoke resistance within the executive branch or Congress. (I shall return to the issue of reorganization in the final chapter.)

Issues of Change Management

As noted in chapter 2, the style of change (as with the F process) can be as important as the substance of change in a reform process. Here I examine change management in foreign aid in the Bush administration, not only for what it tells us about past experience but for the lessons for the future should a future administration choose to reorganize U.S. foreign aid.

What Does the Literature Say?

There is a large literature on managing organizational change in the private sector. We can only point to a few interesting examples here. First, from the scholarly perspective, John Kotter in his *Leading Change* lists a set of principles that are shared by many experts on change management:

- Establishing a sense of urgency
- Creating the guiding coalition
- Developing a vision and strategy
- Communicating the change vision
- Empowering employees for broad-based action
- Generating short-term wins
- Consolidating gains and producing more change
- Anchoring new approaches in the culture[13]

Beginning with a compelling vision, communicating it effectively, creating coalitions of employees supportive of change, demonstrating positive results from change—these are the steps needed to successfully manage change and overcome resistance to change among those affected by it.[14] From the perspective of a highly accomplished corporate leader, key principles of leadership—of which change management is a core component—are similar:

- Without a shared vision that is compelling and truly embraced with passion, it's nearly impossible for any organization to be successful.
- Creating a vision involves deciding where the organization must go, and then, with some passion, communicating (and communicating and communicating) a simple message describing that destination.
- Leadership is as much about listening, about building relationships, about providing encouragement when it's needed, as it is about communicating one's own ideas.

◆ Effective communication is more than simply delivering a collection of well-considered statements. It's also where and how and, above all, when these words are delivered that truly cause messages to take hold and behaviors to change. . . . The real challenge for many leaders is not only communicating per se, it's integrating the way they behave with what they speak and write.

◆ When an organization is engaged in wrenching and fundamental upheaval, it's important that all of the people touched by the organization have something comfortable and familiar to hang on to.[15]

Both of these works implicitly address the issue of style in managing change that has long been a source of debate—should leaders use muscular tactics ("shock and awe") to force acceptance of change, for example, firing or isolating anyone who appears to resist change? Or should the style be more one of persuasion? Much of the current literature appears to come down on the side of the latter.

But to what extent is this literature relevant to change management in the public sector? One of the most famous quotations in public administration, attributed to Wallace Sayre (a professor at Columbia University during the middle of the last century), asserts that "public and private management are fundamentally alike in all unimportant aspects." In what important ways might they be different with regard to managing change?

The key difference is the nature of leadership and authority in the private versus public sectors. Leaders of public organizations have much less authority or power to implement change than private sector leaders do because of legislative restrictions and the political environment in which public sector organizations must function. Thus, change management in public organizations typically requires much more communication, coalition building, negotiation, and time than in private organizations. This difference is probably most evident in the U.S. political system, which is among the most decentralized in the world, with a large role played by Congress and private organizations in major public sector decisions.

The impact of our political institutions on change management can be seen in the nature of public organizations as well as in the role of Congress. U.S. government agencies look like discrete organizations, but they seldom are, especially the many agencies that manage spending programs. For every federal dollar spent, there are interests that support those expenditures because they believe in them or benefit from them. Those interests exist within government agencies (that is, in the bureaus responsible for the particular policies and expenditures), in Congress, and among private organizations and groups who often work together in informal networks. Thus, an effort by an agency head to bring about major changes in a particular program within the agency can—where such changes are unwelcome—quickly provoke resistance from Congress and private groups supporting that program.

In short, government agencies are frequently coalitions of separate interests themselves, tied into broader networks of interests outside government rather than the discrete, hierarchical public organizations they appear in organigrams.[16] Political appointees coming into government leadership positions for the first time often discover this reality the hard way when they collide with those interests.

Additionally, government employees usually cannot be fired if they resist changes proposed by agency leaders. They can be sidelined and isolated—and they can try to mobilize opposition to proposed changes. The rigidities in public employment regulations are there for good reasons— to prevent the politicization of public service and protect the rights of employees. But this arrangement puts another constraint on change management in the public sector—especially for leaders accustomed to the "shock and awe" approaches— that does not exist in the private sector.

A third difference between the public and private sector is the political environment of change. Where legislation is needed for significant changes, Congress must be involved. But even where legislation may not be needed, Congress can become involved if it sees its interests affected. Indeed, some believe that, constitutionally, Congress should be involved in any major organizational changes in the executive branch, whether legislation is required or not.

At a minimum, key members of Congress and their staffs need to be consulted in the planning and implementation of change. They have their own goals, agendas, and practices and the power to protect them. To make matters more complicated, different members and staffers often have differing and conflicting agendas, creating a challenging political minefield for change managers in the executive branch. For those in the executive branch unfamiliar with congressional views, it is especially important to consult, to listen, and—most difficult—to *hear* what members and their staffs say. What they mean is not always evident in what they say. Change managers also need to frame their proposed changes in terms of issues and values Congress will accept, to figure out what is negotiable and what is not, and to build support coalitions for change.

Not surprisingly, it almost always takes time to get a major organizational change through the executive branch and Congress. And then it takes a lot more time and effort to implement major changes, usually with a considerable cost in program dislocation. It is often several years before major organizational reforms can be fully realized and the affected agencies and programs are again running smoothly. The major organizational changes in the Bush administration—the creation of the Department of Homeland Security and the reform of the intelligence agencies—are still being sorted out years after the changes were approved by Congress.

Change Management in the Bush Administration's Aid Initiatives

The F process has become the most ambitious reform in foreign aid undertaken by the Bush administration. It is widely regarded as a failure. What are its lessons for a future administration implementing major changes in foreign aid?

Context is important. With only about two years before the end of Bush's second term, there was a relatively short period to implement such changes given the consulting, planning, explaining, consensus building, and overcoming or overriding resistance within the executive branch, in Congress, and among interest groups. And then, once changes have been approved, there is the time-consuming task of implementing and ironing out the many unexpected issues that arise. The last two years of a two-term administration is an especially difficult time to implement change, where the president is increasingly a lame duck, administration officials are often exhausted (or distracted, looking for their next jobs), bureaucratic interests are entrenched, and a degree of tension and distrust has often built up between an administration and Congress.

Communication is important—and organizational culture plays a role in how information is communicated. Director Tobias consulted frequently and spoke often about his plans for reform. But the style of consultation was often seen as more one of "here is what we are planning; what is your reaction?" rather than "here are some problems we need to address together and here are our ideas; what are yours?" The development community inside USAID and outside it has a culture of consultation, conversation, and consensus rather than discussion and quick decision. This approach undoubtedly reflects the emphasis in much of the community on participation of stakeholders and beneficiaries in development activities on their behalf. This process is time consuming and involves a measure of give and take, but it does make people feel they have had a say and a stake in the decisions that are made (even if they are not the preferred ones). And it involves creating trust on both sides—something that is often a casualty of change management.

Another cultural factor—different from the private sector—is the political nature of agency leadership in the U.S. government. It is a common and well-recognized pattern that incoming political appointees in a new administration—or even newly appointed senior officials in an existing one—often regard the existing crowd of career professionals as tainted by the previous administration, possibly hostile to the new leadership, and even incompetent. Those same incoming political appointees are often regarded by career professionals as yet another lot of arrogant, uninformed, and sometimes incompetent individuals that must be endured until they leave—which sooner or later they always do. These stereotypes and distrust can deepen if they are reinforced by the expected behavior on both sides. And this typically occurs when a new leadership wants to discard past policies and make rapid policy, programmatic, or organizational changes—which they often want to do in foreign aid.

Understanding Congress is another element in change management in Washington. There also seems to have been a misunderstanding of what Congress wanted or would accept in the way of reforms. Congress did want more data. Staff and members were unlikely, however, to give up many earmarks and directives that serve a number of important purposes for them—that is, to force an administration they may distrust to undertake tasks they think necessary and important; to benefit key constituent groups; to help causes they believe in; and to trade for favors by other members. Key members and their staffs felt they had been told about the reforms but were not truly consulted, listened to but not heard. This was a serious failure of communication. Undoubtedly, the rising discontent within USAID with the F process had also been passed on to members of Congress and their staffs, setting off alarms on the Hill about the efficacy and intent of the reforms.

Finally, communication is also about symbols, and here there appear to have been further breakdowns in change management. The reforms were regarded with suspicion by many in Washington who feared they represented a merger by stealth of USAID into the Department of State. That Tobias spent most of his time at the State Department (and took most of USAID's policy and budget shop with him) reinforced this fear. His reduction of USAID's operating expenses and shift of funding from Development Assistance to ESF also reinforced the impression that a takeover was, in fact, under way. Other actions taken—one of USAID's periodic news magazines ceased publication and conferences of USAID mission directors halted—were seen as further evidence that Tobias cared little about the organization or its staff. Whatever the intent of these decisions (Tobias's former staff explain these budgetary decisions in terms of technical adjustments), they were widely regarded as signs of a shift of control of development aid toward State Department political objectives and away from USAID's development mission.

Based on this discussion and the general lessons of change management listed above, what conclusions can we draw about change management in the F process? The F process strategy, with time, had some short-term wins. It produced expanded data on aid expenditures and better coordination in what had been scattered aid programs in USAID and State. But the reform was initiated not as a result of a sense of urgency or crisis on the part of USAID's and State's professional staff and outside constituents, but because the secretary of state decided it made sense. No effective guiding coalition of highly credible change agents drawn from the professional staff within State and USAID worked closely to advise Tobias and to legitimize and implement change. It was not anchored in the cultures of either agency. State Department officers were not used to the planning and programming culture of USAID, where objectives were identified, measurable indicators established, and the metrics of success published. And the F process appeared to override USAID's culture of strong consensual norms. Those designing the reforms appear to have not understood the political constraints they were operating under, especially with Congress. And behavior was not seen to be consistent with the stated intent of elevating development as a purpose in U.S. foreign policy. Given the rising criticism in Congress and among the development community, the reforms appear to have been headed for disaster even before the sudden resignation of Tobias for other reasons.

Summing Up

Organizational changes are difficult, but they are overdue in U.S. aid if the benefits of the Bush transformation in foreign aid are to be realized and the challenges of relief, development, global problems, and failing and failed states facing the United States are to be met effectively. But managing change is never easy. There is no better summary of the challenges of change management than the one offered by Tobias in his book on the topic: "Change is a lot like fire. Manage it, turn it to your advantage, and you will bask in the warmth of its glow; ignore it or manage it poorly, and one thing is certain—eventually you will get burned."[17]

FIVE

U.S. Aid Going Forward

T his book has examined the recent history of U.S. foreign aid. It is now time to turn to the future. Given the Bush administration's efforts to transform aid and the resulting chaos of the past seven years, how should the next administration shape the purposes, policies, and organization of such aid to ensure its future effectiveness? And how should it manage the implementation of needed changes smoothly, avoiding the evident problems of the recent past?

Foreign Aid and the Evolving World of the Twenty-First Century

U.S. foreign aid evolved after the Second World War as an instrument for containing the expansion of Soviet and Chinese influence, first in Europe and then in the developing world. The world of the twentieth century that gave rise to foreign aid is mostly gone. These first few years of the twenty-first century have presented seven new changes that have dramatically affected the purposes, uses, and organization of U.S. aid. They should be taken into consideration in any reconceptualization and reorganization of U.S. aid in the future:

Rise of Terrorism and Asymmetrical Power

The problems of terrorism and the location of sources and sanctuaries for terrorist organizations in fragile states have been explored in chapter 2.

These problems are likely to remain with us for the foreseeable future along with the challenge of developing effective policies and programs to deal with them.

Concentration of Poverty and Problems of Growth in Sub-Saharan Africa

What was called a third world of developing countries in the last half of the twentieth century has broken into disparate parts. Some countries have made remarkable economic progress (for example, Korea, Botswana, and Chile) and no longer need foreign aid. Others, including China and India, with promising rates of growth and poverty reduction, need aid less and less and provide foreign aid themselves—China in particular. While they still have pockets of severe poverty, they are also increasingly capable of dealing with those problems through rapid growth and direct interventions. Where the problems of development are most concentrated and where aid is most needed is in much of sub-Saharan Africa and several other very poor countries in other parts of the world, such as Haiti, Laos, and Bolivia. And the difficulties of development in these countries are as much related to institutions—that is, involving the capacity and quality of governance—as they are to scarce resources. These are the true "third world" countries of the twenty-first century, and they present a continuing and difficult challenge for development and development aid in coming years.

Global Issues and International Public Goods

As noted above, these issues are not new to aid giving. But they will almost certainly become far more prominent in this century with globalization and worldwide economic growth. Fighting HIV/AIDS is already a high priority for U.S. aid giving. Addressing problems of climate change is surely next in line, and this purpose could also absorb large amounts of aid. Water scarcity is another looming transnational problem and potential cause of humanitarian crises, food shortages, and interstate conflict in some of the world's already troubled regions. Continuing population growth, economic development, and the physical and economic integration of the world will likely expand and deepen problems of global public goods throughout the twenty-first century. And many of them are likely to make a claim on foreign aid.

Technological Change

We are living through a revolution in information technology perhaps as important as the industrial revolution of the nineteenth century. It involves not only the creation of worldwide networks of communication through computers and cell phones but the rapidly evolving capabilities of cell phones themselves—from instruments of communication toward mechanisms for photography, banking, medical assessments, market knowledge (even for small farmers in Africa), and other, as yet unimagined, uses. It seems likely that the pace of technological change will continue to be rapid and bring other surprises in the future. Development agencies and development aid should be nimble enough to help exploit those changes for their development potential.

Expansion in the Number and Types of Development Actors

In the twentieth century we thought of governments as the main promoters of development: rich donor countries provided aid to the governments of poor countries to fund agreed programs and projects. That world is long gone. There are now thousands of nongovernmental organizations in both developed and developing countries involved in supporting development. Some, like the faith-based nongovernmental organizations (NGOs) and megachurches in the United States, manage large amounts of private aid as well as flows of public aid from donor governments. Some fall into the category of social entrepreneurs, seeking not just to deliver resources to the needy but to discover sustainable, profit-making ways to improve the human condition. There are an increasing number of philanthropic foundations, large and small, engaged in large-scale aid giving—the Bill and Melinda Gates Foundation being the most prominent but far from the only one. Finally, more and more private enterprises are engaged in good works abroad—at times on their own and at other times in public-private partnerships with governments. Many of these efforts may fail; others may not be what they seem. But there is no doubt that something important has happened in the world of development—a lot more organizations and individuals are involved in aiding development abroad than in the past. U.S. aid will need to be flexible in the future if it is to collaborate with and influence the growing number of actors in international development. The Global Development Alliance, mentioned in chapter 2, is a promising innovation that can be expanded to help engage these opportunities.

New Politics of Aid in the United States

U.S. aid has traditionally rested on a right-left coalition, with those on both sides of the political spectrum supporting it as a useful instrument promoting U.S. security during the cold war (and later, to promote peacemaking in the Middle East). Those on the left were more supportive of using aid to reduce poverty abroad. With the cold war over and economic assistance for Middle East peacekeeping much reduced, the traditional anti-aid right had potentially much less at stake in supporting U.S. aid abroad. But several things have happened in the twenty-first century to change this old political equation. First, the terrorist attack on the United States has given the right a new reason to support aid as a tool in the fight against terrorism. Second, George Bush has sold performance-based aid (that is, from the Millennium Challenge Corporation, MCC) as more effective, addressing one of the objections to aid from the political right in the United States (though this claim has yet to be proven). Third, and perhaps most important, the political right has divided over the aid issue, with many conservative evangelicals increasingly supportive of aid for humanitarian relief, fighting HIV/AIDS, and other activities associated with improving the human condition abroad and especially in Africa. This change could represent a major shift in the politics of aid giving in the United States, providing stronger public support for aid than at any time in the past. In short, the domestic politics of U.S. aid in the twenty-first century may prove to be quite different from those of the last century. These changes will influence how aid is used, as well as how the political coalition supporting it in Congress and beyond is put together and managed.

Hard Power, Soft Power, Smart Power, and the International Politics of Aid

One of the lessons of the first seven years of the twenty-first century is that while the United States has unchallenged world supremacy in military capabilities and the largest and one of the most dynamic world economies, its power to shape world policies is also constrained in important ways. Alone it cannot solve many of the important problems confronting it in a world that is increasingly integrated and interdependent. Soft power— intangible qualities such as reputation, trust, the admiration of other peoples, cultural attractiveness—can make it easier for a nation to persuade other governments and their peoples to adopt desired policies.[1] U.S. aid that benefits others abroad—whether humanitarian relief (as with the Asian tsunami in late 2004), development aid, or assistance in dealing with global problems—is an important element in soft power. In a world where U.S. leadership requires the use of force and pressure, generous foreign aid is a balance to muscular unilateralism, a symbol that the United States cares about interests other than its own. One should not overestimate the impact of aid as soft power—it cannot overcome fundamental differences of values and interests. But it has never been more useful in smoothing the hard edges of worldwide leadership, a role that the United States will surely continue to have for the foreseeable future with generous levels of aid clearly tied to improving the human condition abroad.

These changes in the world of the twenty-first century together argue for a future U.S. aid program that will have at its core a development mission (with development broadly defined as relief, growth, and poverty reduction together with global problems related to development), which will be both an *end* in itself—that is, a reflection of U.S. values of helping others to help themselves—and a *means* to other ends tied to U.S. national interests, for example, fighting terrorism and demonstrating U.S. soft power. A U.S. aid program that is agile and flexible is called for, one that can engage other development actors effectively and exploit new technological opportunities. If such a program can include new domestic groups that support development along with those who have been a traditional part of the development coalition, strong domestic support for aid and development programs could be cemented for the foreseeable future. How do these imperatives and opportunities translate into concrete policy and organizational arrangements?

U.S. Aid Policies and Organization in the Twenty-First Century

If we agree that in the future there are likely to be five main purposes of U.S. aid—providing relief in natural or man-made crises; assisting in development, that is poverty reduction and economic growth; addressing global problems; fighting terrorism; and pursuing other diplomatic and security goals, for example, supporting Middle East peace, countering drug production and crime—we can begin to see the outlines of a rationalized aid organization described in the previous chapter.

Development and addressing global problems involve similar types of activities but from two different angles—the first with a *country focus* including work in multiple sectors, and the second with a *worldwide sector focus,* operating primarily in poor countries that cannot (or will not) address the key global issues on their own. The actual activities funded with the aid might be the same—strengthening health systems, assisting with environmental protection, and providing reliable sources of clean water. Programs addressing development and global issues will call on many of the same professionals and the same programming systems. They should be located in the same aid agency. Relief and development work also overlap; when relief is winding down, it is almost always the case that development work gets under way. They too should be co-located.

Policy decisions involving the country allocation of aid for ends that do not involve development as a primary goal—for example, pursuing diplomatic objectives with aid provided as an incentive or fighting drugs or terrorism in priority countries—should be located in the agencies seeking to achieve these goals. But where that aid is actually used to fund development activities, it should at least be implemented by the development aid agency (wherever it is located bureaucratically), and officials of that agency should have a say in how the aid is used. Figure 5-1 suggests such an arrangement.

To ensure that the development agency is competent to deal with all issues falling within its areas of responsibilities, it will be important that it has the knowledge and technical expertise on staff in trade, finance,

F I G U R E   5 - 1. Structuring U.S. Foreign Aid: A Model

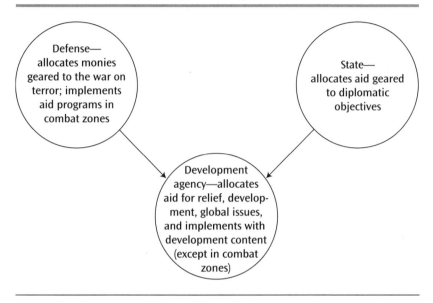

debt, and sector specializations. The U.S. Agency for International Development (USAID) lacks adequate staff and expertise, which has weakened its ability to function as a source for analysis and voice for development inside and outside the government. Indeed, its overall staff has been severely reduced over the past decade with constraints on operating expenses, low staff morale, and a large number of retirements. This is a problem but also an opportunity for the next administration to rebuild a strong aid agency relevant to the needs of the new century. It is noteworthy that the Bush administration has recognized this problem in its proposed aid budget for fiscal year 2009 and has requested a significant increase in funding for operating expenses and personnel for USAID.

The development agency will also need the kind of personnel who can engage collaboratively with other development actors—not just in writing contracts but also working closely with others. It will also need some flexible funds in its annual budgets to permit it to sponsor research and encourage innovation in development practice and to take advantage of new breakthroughs.

A perennial issue regarding the organization of development aid among all donor governments and international institutions is to what extent should there be a field presence of aid officials and what authorities should they have over the use and implementation of aid activities. USAID has long had a strong field staff with considerable delegated authorities to plan and manage U.S. aid. As noted earlier, the apparent shift of these authorities to USAID headquarters in Washington as part of the F process caused much discontent and was seen as weakening the ability of the agency to do its work well.

It is clear that the more ambitious the type of aid intervention in another country, the more important it is to have staff in the country to manage the intervention—a fact that the World Bank and many other agencies have recognized in their operations and organization. Where, for example, aid is used to promote economic and political reforms or to strengthen local institutions, or is planned with direct participation by intended beneficiaries, it is important for officials to have the knowledge and contacts that come from living and working in the country (and speaking the language) for an extended period of time. Where the aid is essentially a cash transfer (as was the case for many years in U.S. aid to Israel) and implemented by reliable, competent, and "clean" partners in the field, a limited presence in country—for example, a development officer in the U.S. embassy or a regional platform to service multiple countries—might be adequate. In short, a field presence can be important, especially in poor countries, but the type and degree of field presence needs to be decided in the context of the nature of aid interventions undertaken by the aid agency.

The big question in the structuring of U.S. aid in the future is, where should the development agency be located bureaucratically? We have touched on the three main alternatives in the previous chapter: a Department of Development; a subcabinet-level aid agency; and full merger of USAID at least into the Department of State. This discussion will examine some concrete ideas and make some recommendations for the future.

A Department of Development would include all major programs of U.S. bilateral relief and development aid: USAID, MCC, the President's Emergency Plan for AIDS Response (PEPFAR), and aid for international migration and refugees (now in the Department of State), U.S. contributions to multilateral development banks, now housed in Treasury, and other smaller development aid programs now in U.S. government departments and agencies. The Department of Development would implement aid for development from the Defense and State departments. If most of the largest of U.S. development aid programs are not folded into a Department of Development, it is difficult to justify its creation at the cabinet level.

The many advantages of a cabinet-level development agency have been recounted in chapter 3. The disadvantages are mainly political: it would take a major effort on the part of a U.S. president to create such a department; programs long established in State and Treasury would have to be moved, presumably in the face of serious resistance by the secretaries of both departments. Members of Congress would have to be persuaded, pressured, or provided incentives to support the legislation needed for such an organizational initiative. This would all take presidential attention and energy, not to mention a well-organized and effective lobbying campaign outside the U.S. government in support of it. And it would probably have to be initiated right at the beginning of a new administration when individuals and interests are less entrenched and when there is usually something of a honeymoon with Congress.

But a look at the urgent and difficult issues likely to be facing the next president—dealing with the war in Iraq and the growing insecurities in Afghanistan, the continuing threat of terrorism and the spread of weapons of mass destruction, an American economy that seems to be sliding into recession, concerns about health care in the United States, about immigration, about education, about the Social Security system, and the looming threats from climate change—suggests that these issues are more likely to take priority over creating a cabinet-level development agency. Indeed, with these other pressing problems, it might well be seen as a serious misstep for a new president to spend a significant amount time and political capital on development issues and organization, even if those too are badly in need of attention.

A second organizational alternative—a "Plan B"—would be to create a subcabinet-level bilateral development agency that combines the largest programs—MCC, USAID, and PEPFAR—into one organization. These three components, each with its own modus operandi and staff, would work best together, taking advantage of their similar synergies while administering their particular programs separately. One minor but potentially contentious issue—the differing salaries among the three programs—would need to be aligned to ensure equity among staff. This new umbrella-type agency could also act as an implementer for development-oriented programs of other departments and agencies, much as a cabinet-level development agency would and much as USAID has done in the past.

There would need to be mechanisms for ensuring that the new agency be coordinated closely with the Department of State in its activities in the field. At a minimum, it could "take policy guidance" from the secretary of state, as USAID has done. It could continue the joint planning process with State, put in place in the F process. However, it would handle the budgets for its components independently but in consultation with State. To formalize a close relationship, it may make sense to adopt the MCC governance model—a board that includes the secretaries of state, Treasury, and defense, and other senior officials from the administration whose agencies may have some engagement with development issues plus several outside representatives (including individuals from the business, philanthropic, and NGO communities).

The board model makes sure that all relevant voices are heard periodically and establishes a formal channel for coordination. Using the MCC board model may also mean that this new agency could be created by amending existing MCC legislation (legislation governing the establishment and authorities of USAID and PEPFAR would also have to be amended) rather than taking on the passage of an entirely new piece of foreign assistance legislation—potentially at a lower cost in terms of time and effort expended with Congress.[2] Neither the model of cabinet department or of subcabinet-level agency would obviate the need for other interagency coordinating mechanisms described in chapter 3. Interagency coordination on development abroad will undoubtedly remain a challenge—probably a growing one—in the foreseeable future.

The advantage of this alternative is that it creates a single major bilateral aid agency dedicated to the overlapping issues of relief, development, and global issues abroad, thus strengthening the profile of development within the administration (though not as much as a cabinet-level development agency would); it reduces to a substantial degree the existing organizational chaos, and it does so at a reasonable political cost. Because it is far less ambitious than the creation of a cabinet-level agency, it would likely require less presidential involvement and so draw less criticism that a new president was spending his or her time and precious political capital on a relatively low priority issue. It could be framed as part of a much needed cleaning up of problematic organizational changes under the Bush administration and part of a new approach to effective, competent government. The timing is promising for a proposed Plan B because both MCC and PEPFAR are up for reauthorization this year or next (which could easily be put off until a new administration takes office).

A third option is to merge USAID completely into the Department of State, leaving MCC as the principal independent bilateral aid agency. This would mean that there would no longer be an administrator of USAID; its personnel would become part of the Department of State's personnel systems, and its budgets would be fully merged with those of State. A decision on whether USAID's foreign service personnel would be made a separate "cone"—administrative specialty—of the Department of State's system would have to be made. A senior person within State—either a second deputy secretary of state or an under secretary—would serve as the director of the remnants of USAID. It would seem likely that USAID's regional bureaus would merge into those of State and its functional specialists would join those in State. Placing USAID units in State bureaus might be cost saving (if duplication of positions in the two agencies is significant—but I have not seen solid evidence that this is the case) and provide maximum policy coherence between U.S. bilateral aid and U.S. foreign policy goals.

This alternative makes sense if greater coherence between USAID's development work and State's diplomatic mission is the first priority of a new administration. But it is likely that a merger would lead to a downgrading of USAID's traditional development mission in favor of urgent diplomatic concerns in the more powerful Department of State, as has been discussed in other chapters. And if Global Health/Child Survival and Development Assistance came to be regarded by Congress and the development community as diplomatic "walking around money" (a term applied to U.S. aid during the 1950s before USAID was established), support for aid would vanish.

When it was originally set up, USAID existed as a separate agency as a result of a "delegation of authority" from the secretary of state. That is, there was no legislative basis for its existence, and it could have been merged or extinguished at the decision of the secretary. In 1998 legislation was passed establishing USAID as a separate agency. But many of its authorities still derive from the secretary of state. This legislation would have to be amended, but that would probably be the only congressional action needed.

However, there would likely be political problems with this alternative: specifically, resistance from those in Congress and the development community who would see a full merger as the beginning of the end of USAID's development mission as well as the end of the agency itself. Judging from the reactions to the F process, this resistance could be significant and powerful, especially now that the development community is aware of the problems and implications of a full merger.

This argument suggests that while the creation of a cabinet-level development agency may be regarded as the ideal alternative by those in the development community, the political costs of that alternative may be unacceptable to a new president. The probable consequences of a full merger between USAID and the Department of State may prove equally unacceptable to members of Congress and outside interests supportive of aid for development. That leaves the middle option as the most attractive from the point of view of needed organizational reform—combining major bilateral aid agencies and programs into one semi-independent sub-cabinet level aid agency—while minimizing the political cost of change.

Change Management

How should a new president initiate the reforms in aid suggested here? First, the sooner reforms are initiated after the inauguration, the better. In the case of aid reform, this would mean that legislation should be ready to go to Congress quickly after the inauguration. That in turn implies that as much of the planning and consultation as possible will have been done during the period between the election in November and inauguration in January. A transition team for development would be required to work hard during this roughly two-month period. The team would also need to work as transparently and inclusively as possible with the aim of having a final plan by mid-January.

At that point, the new president would announce plans for the reorganization and explain why it is urgent and important. Senior posts in aid agencies would be filled with individuals committed to the reorganization (as a requirement of their appointment) or not filled at all until the organization is ready to be implemented. Shepherding needed legislation through Congress will take time and attention; it is essential that there be champions of the reform in key committees (that is, the Senate Foreign Relations Committee, the House Foreign Affairs Committee, and the foreign operations appropriations subcommittees of both houses of Congress).

Coalitions of professional staff from within affected agencies should be created to guide, explain, and give legitimacy to the reforms as they are implemented. If planned and implemented well, an organizational reform of U.S. development aid could make a major improvement in the way the U.S. government addresses international relief, development, and global issues, which are and will be essential to U.S. leadership worldwide in the twenty-first century. In short, the new administration could realize the promise and possibilities of the transformation in foreign aid sought but not achieved by the Bush administration.

Notes

Chapter One

1. *Foreign aid* for the purposes of this book is defined as the transfer of economic resources (loans, grants, or in-kind transfers like food) on concessional terms (with a minimum of 25 percent grant element current value) from one government to another government, international organization, or nongovernmental entity, one purpose of which is to better the human condition in the recipient country. This definition is very close to the one used by the Development Assistance Committee of the OECD, except it does not set a minimum per capita income level for countries receiving foreign aid. Thus, in my definition, aid to Israel and other middle-income countries is included as foreign aid.

2. *Development* is a concept with many meanings—usually sustained economic growth and poverty reduction—but it can also include democratization, social inclusion, strengthening public institutions and capacity, and the opportunity to realize one's full capabilities.

3. See U.S. National Security Strategy, 2002 and 2006 (www.whitehouse.gov/nsc/nss/2002/ and www.whitehouse.gov/nsc/nss/2006/).

4. Other potential public instruments for promoting development abroad include trade policies (trade preferences for exports of developing countries to U.S. markets), policies affecting U.S. foreign investment, and, in recent decades, immigration policies. While there have been some trade policies shaped to further prosperity in poor countries (African Growth and Opportunity Act), these have tended to be limited since trade policy is strongly tied to domestic political interests within the United States.

5. The data on U.S. foreign aid in this study are taken from USAID's website, U.S. Overseas Loans and Grants (Greenbook) (http://qesdb.cdie.org/gbk/index.html). These data cover grants (net obligations) and loans (net authorizations). Where these data are not available, appropriations and disbursement data are

used. The data cover multilateral and bilateral economic aid from all U.S. government agencies. The data are on a U.S. fiscal year basis.

6. The United States is still the largest donor in absolute terms.

7. I am using the term *purposes* here to mean major, discrete objectives of foreign aid that are ends in themselves. These include promoting U.S. diplomatic goals, furthering development, which is both an end in itself and a means to achieve U.S. diplomatic goals, addressing global issues, providing humanitarian relief, supporting economic and political transitions in former socialist countries, promoting democracy (both as an end and a means), preventing and mitigating conflict, strengthening fragile states, and furthering commercial interests. Many of these overlap in the types of activities they involve. Some, such as strengthening fragile states, are as yet limited since we have much to learn about such states and how to influence them. Promotion of commercial interests abroad is not a major driver of U.S. aid.

8. I am not taking sides here in the sterile debate between Jeffrey Sachs and Bill Easterly that, on the one hand, more aid is imperative (a "big push" approach to tackling world poverty) and, on the other, aid has been largely ineffective and should be sharply reduced or eliminated. It is clear that aid is not the solution to all development problems; it can even at times make them worse. Nor is it the case that most aid has clearly failed to realize its development goals. Aid effectiveness depends on who gets it and how it is used and implemented. Greatly increased aid provided to the wrong government or recipient organization (that is, one that lacks the capacity or probity to use it well) is a waste, or worse. And aid can create perverse as well as beneficial incentives if provided in sufficient quantity, another qualifying element in the aid effectiveness debate. But there are many activities important to growth and poverty reduction that can usefully be funded by considerably more aid, as they have been in the past. Thus, if there is a hidden assumption in this book, it is that more aid, wisely used, can be better.

Chapter Two

1. "Near abroad" refers to those countries bordering Russia that had been part of the former Soviet Union and in which Moscow continues to take a special interest.

2. There was an effort by some in government and the scholarly and policy communities to frame environmental and international health issues as security threats to the United States. See, for example, Thomas Homer-Dixon, *Environment, Scarcity and Violence* (Princeton University Press, 2001); see also endnote 19 below. But this view never proved convincing enough to catch on. The tactic reflects a view that if a policy goal can be justified in security terms, it is likely to be much more compelling politically in the U.S. system.

3. U.S. government spending is typically divided into discretionary and mandated categories. The level of the latter type of expenditures, like Social Security, agricultural subsidies, or Medicaid, is required by law. The former expenditures are the choice of the executive branch and Congress. In 2006 roughly one-third of the federal budget was discretionary. Foreign aid represented 4 percent of discretionary spending with defense and domestic expenditures making up the remaining 96 percent. See Congressional Budget Office data (www.cbo.gov/budget/data/historical.xls).

4. A recent trip report by staff of the Senate Foreign Relations Committee observed, "USAID may be viewed as the neglected stepchild in DC but in the field it is clear that USAID plays either the designated hitter or the indispensable utility infielder for almost all foreign assistance launched from post." See *Embassies Grapple to Guide Foreign Aid,* report to the Committee on Foreign Relations, U.S. Senate, 2007, p. 2.

5. Actually, raiding the aid budget was my informal job description as a deputy assistant secretary of state for Africa, and I was not alone.

6. The trend toward fragmentation was also driven by globalization and the realization that it was difficult to deal with environmental, health, or energy issues at home without addressing those same issues abroad. Secretaries in most federal departments preferred to control their own monies rather than place them in USAID or have to request expenditures abroad from USAID. Criticisms of USAID in Washington made these decisions easier, and neither OMB nor the White House resisted them (nor were they necessarily aware at the leadership level of their existence).

7. Relatively little has been written about the IDCA effort. For a brief history, see Vernon Ruttan, *United States Development Assistance Policy* (Johns Hopkins University Press, 1996), pp. 119–20. This book is the best history of U.S. aid.

8. Perhaps the most influential statement of this concept of how and why policies suddenly change is by John Kingdon in his book *Agendas, Alternatives, and Public Policies* (New York: HarperCollins College Publishers, 1995). Arguably another policy window opened on aid in the years following 9/11 during which the Bush administration could get most of what it wanted out of Congress. But it did not have an overall concept of what it wanted to do with U.S. aid at that time. The window appears now to be closed.

9. I am not aware of any published records of this; but I was USAID deputy administrator at the time, and since it was my idea and I pushed it with the vice president and his study group, I must serve as the primary source for this fact.

10. One small change was that USAID returned to the earlier practice of sending its budget to OMB through the secretary of state. But it also continued to send it directly to OMB as well.

11. He did win in another area: two other agencies, the Arms Control and Disarmament Agency and the U.S. Information Agency, were both folded into the Department of State.

12. Development Assistance Committee, Organization for Economic Cooperation and Development, *The United States,* Paris, 2006 (www.oecd.org/dataoecd/61/57/37885999.pdf).

13. Personal correspondence with Patrick Cronin, who was with USAID in the early years of the Bush administration.

14. See "MCA Monitor Analysis" on the Center for Global Development website for history and commentary on the MCC and MCA (www.cgdev.org/content/publications/?type=63). See also Steve Radelet, "The Millennium Challenge Account in Africa: Promises vs. Progress," testimony before the House Committee on Foreign Affairs, June 28, 2007; Sarah Lucas, "Lessons from Seven Countries: Reflections on the Millennium Challenge Account," April 2007. Both of these documents are available on the Center for Global Development website (www.cgdev.org). See also David Gootnick, "Millennium Challenge Corporation: Progress and Challenges with Compacts in Africa," testimony before the Subcommittee on Africa and Global Health, Committee on Foreign Affairs, House of Representatives, June 28, 2007 (www.gao.gov/new.items/d05625t.pdf).

15. Data come from the MCC website, "Countries" (www.mcc.gov/countries/index.php).

16. Senate Report 110–128, *Department of State, Foreign Operations and Related Programs Appropriations Bill, 2008* (http://thomas.loc.gov/cgi-bin/cpquery/R?cp110:FLD010:@1(sr128), June 2007). Only eleven compacts had been signed at the time of publication of this report. Several more were added in 2007. While there are differences among the experts on the MCC on how spending should be regarded (for example, commitments versus disbursements), it is hard to argue against the implicit assumption on the part of Congress that it is disbursements that count—action rather than intention—and that these have not only been slow by any measure but have been well below planned levels in MCC compacts. It is widely expected that disbursements will pick up as the MCC gains more experience, as needed institutions are put in place in recipient countries, and as expenditures commence. But only time will tell.

17. As a number of experts on PEPFAR have pointed out to me, this last announcing of doubling funding to $30 billion over five years was less than it seemed since Congress was already appropriating $6 billion per year for the program, which if continued over five years would amount to more than $30 billion. For policy analysis of PEPFAR's activities, see the Center for Global Development, *HIV/AIDS Monitor* (www.cgdev.org/section/initiatives/_active/hivmonitor) and PEPFAR Watch (www.pepfarwatch.org/).

18. Center for Strategic and International Studies, "PEPFAR Reauthorization: Looking Forward," transcript of discussion, p. 13 (www.kaisernetwork.org/health_cast/hcast_index.cfm?display=detail&hc=2145).

19. For an excellent analysis of the politics of PEPFAR, see John W. Dietrich, "The Politics of PEPFAR: The President's Emergency Plan for AIDS Relief," *Ethics*

and International Affairs 21, no. 3 (Fall 2007): 277–92 (www.cceia.org/resources/journal/21_3/essay/001.html).

20. Randall Tobias, "The New Approach to U.S. Foreign Assistance," remarks at Woodrow Wilson International Center for Scholars Gala, Washington, D.C., November 17, 2006 (www.state.gov/f/releases/remarks2006/78284.htm).

21. The F framework was somewhat different from the USAID framework, but the approach of classifying countries according to their economic conditions and shaping aid to address those conditions was the same. The white paper can be found at USAID's website (www.usaid.gov/policy/pdabz3221.pdf).

22. Department of State, "Framework for U.S. Foreign Assistance" (www.state.gov/f/c23053.htm).

23. Tobias reportedly indicated this intention in an e-mail to USAID staff toward the end of his tenure.

24. "To reduce widespread poverty" was added to this statement later as a result of pressure from the NGO community who regarded its absence as a sign that the administration had downgraded this element in aid giving.

25. In the view of a number of political scientists, at least. This author is among the skeptics of this theory because of definitional and data problems. But whether right or wrong, it was a useful theory for U.S. presidents to justify their policies promoting democracy abroad in terms of U.S. security interests as well as values.

26. See, for example, the statement of Senator Patrick Leahy at the hearing of the Subcommittee on State, Foreign Operations, and Related Programs of the Senate Appropriations Committee on the FY 2008 USAID Budget Request and Foreign Aid Reform, March 28, 2007.

27. According to Laura Wilson, a senior staffer in F, the first of these decisions made by Tobias was not intended to decrease aid for development but shift development assistance into ESF to achieve greater flexibility and impact since ESF monies, some of which were also used to further development, are less circumscribed by congressional earmarks and directives. But those concerned about the shift pointed out that a future director of U.S. foreign assistance or the secretary of state may allocate ESF primarily for security purposes (which was the original intent for ESF monies), leaving aid for development purposes significantly diminished. Rightly or wrongly, the possible future impact and symbolism of this shift heightened fears that development was being downgraded in the F process. The decision on increasing State's operating expenses was not made by Tobias or his staff. While the reduction in USAID's operating expenses was a decision made by Tobias and provoked criticisms within USAID and Congress, the growing number of critics of the F process saw these decisions together as indications of the downgrading of the role of USAID and development in favor of State Department and the diplomatic uses of aid.

28. Remarks at Society for International Development annual dinner, June 6, 2007.

29. Michael Phillips, "Big Aid Agency Group Splits with Bush," *Wall Street Journal* (online), "Washington Wire," May 11, 2007.

30. Glenn Kessler, "Hill, Aid Groups: One Opaque System Replaced Another," *Washington Post,* July 22, 2007, p. A4.

31. These documents have been regarded as sensitive and so not available to the public, or scholars, for perusal.

32. Staff working with Tobias describe some sixty meetings with congressional staff and members, with a considerable amount of exchange of views and changes in reform plans. Given the criticisms from Representatives Lantos and Lowey and Senators Leahy and Menendez, it is clear that something went wrong in the communication with Congress—it seems unlikely that the public criticisms of Tobias and the reforms were simply partisan sniping.

33. Senator Robert Menendez, "Opening Statement," hearing on confirmation of Henrietta Fore as USAID administrator and director of U.S. Foreign Assistance, June 12, 2007, before the Senate Committee on Foreign Relations (http://menendez.senate.gov/newsroom/record.cfm?id=276585).

34. Tobias and his staff were already in the process of analyzing and adjusting the processes they put into place when he departed USAID. See the "After Action Report," May 2007 (www.state.gov/f/releases/factsheets2007/84579.htm).

35. OECD, *The United States: Development Assistance Committee* (Paris, 2006).

36. Defense Department Directive 3000.05, p. 2, November 28, 2005 (www.dtic.mil/WHS/directives/corres/htm/300005.htm).

37. Quadrennial Defense Review for 2006–09, p. 75 (www.defenselink.mil/gdr/).

38. There were some problems in the implementation of these new authorities at first though coordination between DoD and other agencies improved in 2007. For an account of this and other issues involving the use of economic assistance by the Department of Defense, see the excellent report by J. Stephen Morrison and Kathleen Hicks (project directors) from the Center for Strategic and International Studies, *Integrating 21st Century Development and Security Assistance,* December 2007 (www.csis.org/media/csis/pubs/071211_integratinglowres.pdf).

39. For details on the DoD budget for the global war on terror, see Gordon Adams, "Budgeting for Iraq and the GWOT," testimony before Committee on the Budget of the United States Senate, February 6, 2007 (http://budget.senate.gov/republican/hearingarchive/testimonies/2007/2007-02-06Adams.pdf).

40. Stewart Patrick and Kaysie Brown, "The Pentagon and Global Development: Making Sense of the DoD's Expanding Role," Working Paper 131 (Washington: Center for Global Development, November 2007), p. 6 (www.cgdev.org/content/general/detail/14815). This is another excellent account of DoD's growing role in development and the issues it raises. According to this essay, while the PRTs have been praised in some quarters, others have raised questions about the degree of interagency collaboration they represent and their effectiveness.

41. See www.c6f.navy.mil/APS/.

42. Lauren Ploch, "Africa Command: U.S. Strategic Interests and the Role of the U.S. Military in Africa," Congressional Research Service Report for Congress (Washington: Library of Congress, July 2007), p. 2 (www.fas.org/sgp/crs/natsec/RL34003.pdf).

43. Stephanie Hanson, "The Pentagon's New Africa Command" (New York: Council on Foreign Relations, May 3, 2007), p. 2 (www.cfr.org/publication/13255/).

44. See Secretary of Defense Robert Gates, "Landon Lecture," Kansas State University, November 26, 2007 (www.defenselink.mil/speeches/speech.aspx?speechid=1199).

45. See S/CRS website at www.state.gov/s/crs/.

46. Mark Hanin, "Civilian Reserve Corps," Non-Military Capacity Project Background Paper, Bipartisan Policy Center, August 2007, photocopy, p. 3.

47. See, for example, John De Pauw and George Luz, eds., *Winning the Peace: The Strategic Implications of Military Civic Action* (New York: Praeger 1991).

48. Quoted from a former U.S. Army captain who had served in Iraq in Corine Hegland, "National Security—Why Civilians Instead of Soldiers?" *National Journal,* April 28, 2007, p. 3.

Chapter Three

1. Growth and poverty reduction are, of course, tied together. Sustained growth usually reduces poverty, and the more equitable incomes are at the beginning of a growth phase, the faster poverty is reduced. Actions to reduce poverty directly through expanding education, health services, credit available to the poor, and other activities touching the poor directly can also promote growth. Indeed, the basic services that benefit the poor are the foundations of long-term growth. But the emphases on growth and poverty reduction are different, often reflecting quite different views of what it takes to produce broad-based economic progress, and the constituents of these two approaches have tended to be different.

2. Paul Collier, *The Bottom Billion* (Oxford University Press, 2007).

3. For a review of the literature on the impact of aid on growth, see Michael Clemens, Steve Radelet and Rakhin Bhavnani, "Counting Chickens when they Hatch: The Short Term Impact of Aid on Growth,"Working Paper 44 (Washington: Center for Global Development, 2004). See also Carl-Johan Dalgaard and Henrik Hansen, "On Aid, Growth and Good Policies," *Journal of Development Studies* 37, no. 6 (2001): 17–41.

4. For some early evidence of an "MCC effect," see Doug Johnson and Tristan Azjone, "Can Foreign Aid Create an Incentive for Good Governance? Evidence from the Millennium Challenge Corporation," April 11, 2006, Harvard

University (http://papers.ssrn.com/sol3/papers.cfm?abstract_id=896293). There are numerous anecdotes of the "MCC effect," but this appears to be the only systematic study of that effect. Further studies will be necessary to demonstrate that effect convincingly.

5. Raj Atluru, partner, Draper, Fisher, Jervetson (venture capitalist firm), personal communication; James W. Fox, *The Venture Capital Mirage*, USAID Program and Operations Assessment Report No. 17, August 1996, p. 4, www.usaid. gov/pubs/usaid_eval/pdf_docs/pnaby220.

6. Operations Evaluation Department (OED), "Evaluation Results," *Annual Review of Development Effectiveness* (ARDE), vol. 2 (Washington: World Bank, 1995), p. 41. OED is now called the Independent Evaluation Group within the World Bank.

7. U.K. Department for International Development, "Project Completion Reports: A Review of Findings from Projects Approved between 1986 and 1999," EV637, UK Government, London, 2001, p. 16.

8. OED, ARDE, 2001, p. 62.

9. A "big push" argument today for large amounts of aid to overcome the obstacles to development can be found in Jeffrey Sachs, *The End of Poverty: Economic Possibilities for Our Time* (New York: Penguin, 2005).

10. For an overview of this research, see Clemens, Radelet, and Bhavnani, "Counting Chickens."

11. See www.whitehouse.gov/nsc/nss.pdf.

12. USAID, "Fragile States Strategy," January 2005 (www.usaid.gov/policy/ 2005_fragile_states_strategy.pdf).

13. Diana Cammack, Dinah McLeod, and Alina Rocha Menocal, with Karin Christiansen, *Donors and the "Fragile States" Agenda: A Survey of Current Thinking and Practice* (London: Overseas Development Institute, 2006), p. ix (www.odi. org.uk/events/horizons_nov06/15Dec/JICA percent20Report.pdf). In the view of some, the political and civil rights expected of fully operative states and a measure of legitimacy in the eyes of their citizens are also part of the functionality of states. See Robert Rotberg, *When States Fail* (Princeton University Press, 2004).

14. See, for example, Commission on Weak States and U.S. National Security, *On the Brink: Weak States and U.S. National Security* (Washington: Center for Global Development, 2004).

15. This effort has produced a considerable amount of data and several major reports. See Daniel C. Esty and others, "The State Failure Project: Early Warning Research for U.S. Foreign Policy Planning," in *Preventive Measures: Building Risk Assessment and Crisis Early Warning Systems,* edited by John L. Davies and Ted Robert Gurr, chapter 3 (Boulder, Colo.: Rowman and Littlefield, 1998); Daniel C. Esty and others, *Working Papers: State Failure Task Force Report,* Phase 1 report (McLean, Va.: Science Applications International Corporation, November

30, 1995); Daniel C. Esty and others, *State Failure Task Force Report: Phase II Findings* (McLean, Va.: Science Applications International Corporation, July 31, 1998). Also published as State Failure Task Force, "State Failure Task Force Report: Phase II Findings," in *Environmental Change and Security Project Report,* Phase 2 report (Washington: Woodrow Wilson Center, Summer 1999); Jack A. Goldstone and others, in consultation with Matthew Christenson and others, *State Failure Task Force Report: Phase III Findings* (McLean, Va.: Science Applications International Corporation, September 30, 2000); Robert H. Bates and others, *Political Instability Task Force Report: Phase IV Findings* (McLean, Va.: Science Applications International Corporation, 2003).

16. Global Development Alliance, *The Development Frontier,* USAID, September 2007, p. 1 (www.usaid.gov/our_work/global_partnerships/gda/newsletter/sept07.pdf).

Chapter Four

1. See the Commission on the Organization of the Executive Branch of Government, *Report to Congress,* vol. I (Washington: Government Printing Office, 1949), pp. 32 and 34.

2. See, for example, Luther Gulick, "Notes on the Theory of Organization," in *Classics of Public Administration,* edited by Jay Shafritz, Albert Hyde, and Sandra Parkes (Belmont, Calif.: Thompson Wadsworth, 2004), pp. 90–104.

3. For a discussion of theories of public management, see Harold Seidman and Robert Gilmour, *Politics, Position and Power* (Oxford University Press, 1986). The authors observe that some organizations—for example, the Heritage Foundation—have advocated duplication for the competition it can generate. But, they conclude, "It is easy to pick out the flaws in the concepts of unity of command, straight lines of authority and accountability and organization by major purpose; it is far more difficult to develop acceptable alternatives" (p. 3).

4. Former U.S. ambassador to Egypt Edward Walker remarked, "Aid offers an easy way out for Egypt to avoid reform. They use the money to support antiquated programs and to resist reforms" (Charles Levinson, "$50 billion Later: Taking Stock of U.S. Aid to Egypt," *Christian Science Monitor,* April 12, 2004 [www.csmonitor.com/2004/0412/p07s01-wome.html]). See also Robert Zimmerman, *Dollars, Diplomacy and Dependency: Dilemmas of U.S. Economic Aid* (Boulder, Colo.: Lynne Rienner, 1993) for an exposition of this view.

5. By unifying all its major development programs and policy and implementation responsibilities into one agency, the British government has, in the view of many, created the most coherent development aid organization among all major aid donors.

6. This is the story of the Ministry of Development in Germany, originally set up in 1961 with almost no visibility or even responsibility over German aid. Over the decades, with a succession of effective ministers, it has gained control over most of German aid and is a prominent and visible element in the German government and the prominent player in German aid policies. See Carol Lancaster, *Foreign Aid: Diplomacy, Development, Domestic Politics* (University of Chicago Press, 2006).

7. The majority of the members of the HELP Commission, whose report, *Beyond Assistance,* was recently published, supported the creation of an International Affairs Department with four subcabinet agencies reporting to the secretary: one for trade and development, one for humanitarian affairs, one for political and security issues, and one for public diplomacy. The department would have regional platforms staffed by officers of each of the four agencies. This model is based on the organization of DoD. The question is where would control over the budgets, personnel, and policies of the four subcabinet-level agencies rest and how consistent is the rest of the model with the requirements of managing U.S. relations with foreign countries (which are much more the key focal point of U.S. foreign policy than regions as in DoD) to achieve multiple goals. Nevertheless, it is an intriguing model and worth considering in more detail. But a radical restructuring of U.S. foreign affairs agencies is well beyond the scope of this book.

8. See Stewart Patrick and Kaysie Brown, *Greater than the Sum of Its Parts? Assessing "Whole of Government" Approaches to Fragile States* (New York: International Peace Academy, 2007). Patrick and Brown do not find many cases of effective "whole of government" coordinating mechanisms for addressing fragile states.

9. I wish to thank Gordon Adams from American University for bringing the NTCT to my attention.

10. See the NCTC website, www.nctc.gov/about_us/what_we_do.html.

11. See the DoD website, www.defenselink.mil/qdr/.

12. Terry Moe, "The Politics of Bureaucratic Structure," in *Can the Government Govern?* edited by John Chubb and Paul Peterson (Brookings, 1989), p. 268.

13. John P. Kotter, *Leading Change* (Boston: Harvard Business School Press, 1996), pp. 21–22. This list comprises the titles of the chapters in his book.

14. One expert on change in the public sector argues on the basis of a major case study that resistance to change is not automatic or necessarily crippling. A shared sense of the need for change, and effective communication by and trust in those leading change, can be effective in smoothing shifts in policies, programs, and organization. See Steven Kelman, *Unleashing Change: A Study of Organizational Renewal in Government* (Brookings, 2005).

15. Randall Tobias, *Put the Moose on the Table: Lessons in Leadership from a CEO's Journey through Business and Life* (Indiana University Press, 2003), pp. 246–53. The intriguing question, which only Tobias can answer, is why did his

approach to change management in the F process differ so much from the guidelines he suggests in his own book on the subject?

16. In the past, the tight relationships between U.S. government agencies, their congressional committee members and staffs, and private interests were called "iron triangles." See Hugh Heclo, "Issue Networks and the Executive Establishment," in *The New American Political System,* edited by Anthony King (Washington: American Enterprise Institute Press, 1978), pp. 87–124. This term has morphed into "networks" as the ties between these political actors have loosened. But no one argues these networks are not still present and highly influential, especially when change is in the air.

17. Tobias, *Put the Moose on the Table,* p. 251. The mystery remains why Tobias did not follow his own excellent advice.

Chapter Five

1. Combining hard and soft power is increasingly called *smart power.* See, for example, the Center for Strategic and International Studies, Commission on Smart Power (www.csis.org/smartpower/).

2. The extent of these changes is a work for lawyers. In the judgment of experts on aid legislation, this approach would at least be less complicated than the efforts to reorganize the intelligence community during the Bush administration. (Personal correspondence, June 11–12, 2007, with Robert Lester, former USAID lawyer and drafter of aid legislation.)

Index